the
Pretty Good
Jim's
Journal
Treasury

The Definitive Collection of Every Published Cartoon

by Jim

Andrews McMeel
Publishing

Kansas City

Other Books by Jim

I Went to College and it was okay
I Got a Job and it wasn't that bad
I Made Some Brownies and they were pretty good
I Got Married if you can believe that
I Feel Like a Grown-up Now

www.andrewsmcmeel.com

99 00 01 02 03 BAH 10 9 8 7 6 5 4 3 2 1

ISBN: 0-7407-0007-3

Library of Congress Catalog Card Number: 99-61209

This Book

It may seem silly to publish a treasury of a comic strip that most people have never heard of. Even I think it's kind of silly, and I'm the author.

Jim's Journal, in its heyday, ran in a few dozen college newspapers. The five book collections have sold maybe 60,000 copies. They tell me that's not too shabby in the world of book publishing, but normally, if you're releasing a treasury, you've done a lot better than that. The only other treasuries I can think of offhand are *Calvin and Hobbes* and *The Far Side*, comic strips that ran in thousands of major daily newspapers, sold millions of books, and were known and beloved pretty much the world over.

So, I consider myself lucky to humbly present this *Jim's Journal* treasury.

And while it may baffle the uninitiated, I hope fans of *Jim's Journal* will like it. In fact, if you're a fan of *Jim's Journal*, why don't you consider this book my personal gift to you—a hearty thanks for liking my comic strip. (This is a very special kind of gift, in that you have to pay $14.95 for it.)

To this day, when I meet someone and tell them that I used to do a comic strip called *Jim's Journal*, four times out of five they'll tell me they've never heard of it. But that one time out of five, the person will get wide-eyed, smile, and say *"You're* Jim? I *love* Jim!" and proceed to tell me how Jim was like a friend, and reading his little journal in the newspaper was a great way to start every day.

So, I dedicate this book to Jim's fans. You're the people who made my experience of being a cartoonist a rewarding one.

The life of a cartoonist can get pretty lonely. With the exception of an occasional book signing, I was basically just working at home alone all the time, with no idea whether anybody was out there.

So, thanks for noticing.

—Scott Dikkers ("Jim")

I'm Jim.
This is the
journal of my
day-to-day life.

I Went to College and it was okay

The first *Jim's Journal* book I published was *I Went to College and it was okay*. I self-published it, and hand-delivered it to stores for almost a year before Andrews McMeel called me one day to ask if they could publish it. I guess they had heard it was selling pretty well. I was happy to be out of the publishing business. All that dealing with ISBN numbers, UPC symbols, and printing presses was eating away at my soul. I really just wanted to write and draw.

The book was a collection of my daily comic strip, which I had been doing for about two years in the University of Wisconsin's *Daily Cardinal* newspaper.

In those first years, Jim was a college student, as were most of his readers. So, I decided the nominal theme of his first book should be his college experience.

I, on the other hand, had recently dropped out of college with no intention of returning.

I went to the University of Wisconsin—River Falls, the University of Bridgeport, and the University of Southern California. It was at USC that I came up with the concept for *Jim's Journal*, but I didn't publish any Jim comics until I moved to Madison, Wisconsin, where I wasn't even going to school.

The specific college Jim attended is never named. Most colleges are pretty much the same, so I decided it really didn't matter where he went to school. I often imagined Jim attended Carleton College, just because it seemed so typical and pastoral. Sometimes I drew Madison in the background. But most of the time, Jim existed only on an imaginary cartoon campus that had no relation to any real place.

Most of the classes Jim attended were made-up, but some were based on real ones of mine, like creative writing.

In the strip, Jim never really graduates. He just sort of stops going eventually. And that pretty much happened to me, too. I just got sick of going to college. And pretty soon after, I got sick of Jim going to college, too.

Fall Semester

Freshman Year

Today was my first day at college.	I had a big envelope filled with maps and brochures the school sent me.	I used them to find my way to my dorm, the cafeteria, and other places.	After walking around all day I went to my dorm room and just sat there.

I met my room-mate today. His name is Tony.	He came in our room and said, "Decent, decent," while he looked around.	He said his brother was in college and told him all about dorms.	We could've been assigned to places a lot worse than this, Tony said.

I went to my first class today. It was American Literature.

Somebody next to me asked me if I had a pen.

I said I didn't have an extra one, so he asked somebody else.

The professor told us to read a whole book by Friday.

I had two more classes today.

I'm supposed to read two or three textbook chapters for each of them.

Tonight Tony went down to the dorm lounge to play pool while I read.

I only read one and a half chapters and started getting really tired.

Last night my roommate Tony stumbled in at about 2 a.m.

He threw up and then passed out.

This morning he got up and told me this is what Hell would be like.

He also said he had a pretty good time.

Yesterday in my philosophy class we learned all about Karl Marx.

It was pretty interesting.

For the rest of the day I thought about Marxism and thought it was a good philosophy.

But the next day I was back to my regular self.

Today I slept in and missed my geology class.

I was tired all day.

But later I got in front of the TV.

I had a box of Hostess Cupcakes and a bottle of Coke and I felt fine.

I bought a pack of Nutter Butters yesterday.

When I got up this morning they were all gone.

My roommate Tony said, "I didn't know they were yours—I'll buy you another pack."

He got me some Chips Ahoy.

I guess he thinks cookies are cookies. I don't, but I like Chips Ahoy anyway.

Yesterday I was bored.

So I took a bus to the mall.

I spent all day looking around in the book stores, record stores, and gift shops.

Today when I woke up my legs were sore.

I didn't do anything today.

I took a walk around campus last night.

I saw a couple people from one of my classes.

But they didn't recognize me.

Tony's right. He's always saying I need to get out and meet people.

I decided a job is a good way to meet some new people.

I went to McDonald's and filled out an application.

I was hired right away and a guy showed me how to put fries in their little bags.

His name was Mark or Matt or something like that.

I worked all day. I must've bagged a million fries.

I only worked a couple hours at my new job over the weekend.

But today I was back to work bagging fries.

I even learned to heat fish fillet buns.

The manager says it won't be long before I'm flipping hamburgers.

Here are some of the people I've met while working at McDonald's:

Ruth. She's always in a good mood.

Mark. He's been here 4 years and has never gotten a raise.

I think he's bitter about it.

Steve. He's the manager. He has an odd reverence for McDonald's.

9

I couldn't get to sleep last night. 	I kept thinking I still had to bag fries. 	So I watched an old movie on TV. 	Tony thinks I should quit my job at McDonald's.  But I kinda like it.
I stayed home all day today. 	I think I'm coming down with a cold. 	My throat is sore. I hate that. 	I think sore throats are the worst thing there is. 
I knew it. I have a cold. 	I look like this. 	But I feel like this. 	I hate colds. 
I've been taking a lot of cold medicine. 	I feel like a giant bottle of Liquid Comtrex. 	That stuff tastes terrible. 	And it only makes me feel better for a couple hours. 

There's only one good thing about having a cold.

It makes you appreciate when you're healthy.

I was feeling a lot better today. I went to work and school.

When I got home, Tony was coughing and sniffling. It looks like he has a cold now.

I ran into Ruth today. She works at McDonald's with me.

She looked different out of uniform.

We'd never talked outside of work before.

We didn't seem to know what to say to each other.

Last night I went to a movie with Tony and his friends.

It was pretty good.

Today at McDonald's I learned to work the cash register.

I was really slow—too many buttons to remember.

Customers probably thought I was sort of stupid.

I felt sort of stupid for the rest of the day.

I had a test in my geology class today.

Before class everybody was going over notes and quizzing each other.

I got a little nervous because I didn't know half of what they were talking about.

But the test wasn't so bad, and I think I did okay.

Tony came into McDonald's today.

I'm not sure why, but I was embarrassed when I saw him.

He said I looked like an organ grinder's monkey, and that didn't help.

Incidentally, Tony ordered a Big Mac, fries, and a Coke.

(that's what everybody orders)

I crammed for a test all morning.

Then I took the test.

I could've done a lot better.

I have another test tomorrow, but I can study for it in the morning.

I had a lot of tests this week... My brain is exhausted.

On my way home today I saw a guy playing his saxophone on the sidewalk.

I sat and listened to him.

It was just what I needed.

Last night I was sitting around when I thought of how good a pizza would taste.

I called to have one delivered, but it never came.

I called again and they said it would be late, but with $2 off.

It came a half hour later. It was practically cold.

I should've made a peanut-butter sandwich.

I spent most of my day in the library.

I was there to read "The Sound and the Fury" for my literature class.

Then I came home and watched TV.

TV seemed a lot more stupid than it usually does.

All I could think about today was sleep.

I stayed up till 6am. last night writing a paper.

I forgot about it till the last minute.

It's probably the worst paper I've ever written.

I got a B on that paper I wrote the other night.

Maybe I should write all my papers in a last-minute rush.

I think they come out better that way.

Today I bought some of those straw-berry Newtons.

They were pretty good.

I went home for Thanksgiving. 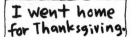	I ate a lot and saw a lot of relatives that I hadn't seen in a while.	I hung around with my hometown friends too. 	But that wasn't quite like it used to be. 

Today Tony asked me to write a paper for him. 	I refused, but he kept asking me. 	"It's the principle of the thing," I kept saying. 	I actually considered doing it when he offered me $50.  But I have enough of my own work to do.

Tony's term paper was due today. 	Yesterday I told him I wouldn't write it for him—even though he said he'd pay me. 	So he stayed up late writing it himself, occasionally asking for my help. 	This morning, before he woke up, I read it. I felt sorry for him. It was pretty bad.

I got up late today. 	I tried to get to my first class on time. 	But while walking to it I realized I'd already missed half of it, so I decided not to go. 	The rest of the day seemed to go by in no time. 

I felt like doing something different today. 	So I walked by the lake.  DIKKERS	I almost froze after only a few minutes. 	I went to the bookstore instead.  I just browsed, like I always do.
A guy came into McDonald's today and didn't order any food.	He just asked for a handful of ketchup. 	He comes in a lot.  DIKKERS	He probably saves a lot of money on ketchup. 
I have my final exams this week. 	I took one this morning. It wasn't too bad.  DIKKERS	I came home and ate some doughnuts and watched TV. 	Tony told me he has two final exams at the same time tomorrow.
I went back to my hometown today. 	My mom said, "Hi, Jim."  DIKKERS	She said Miles Fikema got married, and I didn't know what she was talking about. 	Then I remembered that the Fikemas were one of our neighbors. 

Today I slept till noon.

I got up and looked out the window.

I went downstairs to make some breakfast. My mom had a lot of food.

My grandma visited today from Oregon.

She brought presents and fudge.

I ate so much fudge that I didn't feel like eating anything else all day.

My grandma asked me all about what I was taking in school.

Today was New Year's Day.

Tony called me.

"Hey, happy New Year, Jim!" he said.

He told me all about what he did to celebrate last night.

It's nice not having any homework to do.

It snowed today.

My mom said she liked having me around so I could shovel the driveway.

Even though it was cold, I got so warm shoveling that I took my coat off.

Spring Semester

Freshman Year

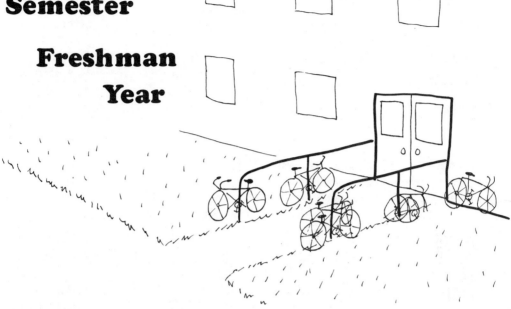

I came back to school today.

I watched TV all day.

Later at night I went to the grocery store... I felt like a zombie.

I have a class with Mark, who works at McDonald's with me.

I feel uneasy around Mark.

He always points out the dreary, hopeless aspect of everything.

I think he just does it to be funny, but I'm not sure.

I had a shake-spearean drama class today.

I came late & forgot my book and notebook.

I borrowed a pen from somebody and took notes on the back of my syllabus.

When I got home I couldn't find the notes I took.

Tony started a new weight-lifting regime last night.

It was peaceful while he was at the gym.

I got a lot of reading done.

When he came back he said he lifted weights for 2½ hours and felt great.

This morning he could barely move.

I don't think he even went to his classes today.

Today I went to class, worked at McDonald's, etc...

It was an average day.

Tony was feeling well enough today to hobble to class.

He says he'll never lift weights again.

After my classes today I started a story for my creative-writing class.

The story isn't due till next Wednesday, but I had an idea for it today.

It's a science-fiction story in which everything in the universe disappears.

But I can't think of where to take it from there.

A couple of guys asked for job applications at McDonald's today.

They laughed hysterically while they filled them out.

They used silly pseudonyms and wrote "Pope" for previous employment and things like that.

Steve, the manager, was angry. He threw the applications away.

I thought they were pretty funny.

At work today I spent most of my time mopping the floor.

I didn't think I'd exerted myself very much,

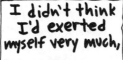

but when I got home I was exhausted.

I ran into Sam today. He works at McDonald's.

He wanted me to work for him tomorrow night.

I told him I couldn't because I was already working then.

I felt sorry for him. He said he'd miss a quiz if he had to work.

I did my laundry today.

There are washers and dryers in the basement of where I live.

Somebody else was finishing up a load while I waited for mine.

He took his clothes out of the dryer and folded them really neatly.

I felt like doing something different today.	So I got on a bus and went around the route a couple times.	All the bumping around made me tired.	
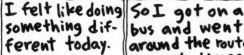

I wasn't in the mood to be in school today.	The professors might as well've been reading the phone book to me. I just wasn't interested.	I came home and took a nap—something I hardly ever do.	When I got up I felt energetic and creative. I stayed up till 3 a.m. reading Trivial Pursuit answers.

Today in my writing class Mark read his story aloud.	Everyone thought it needed some revising.	Mark told me later that he'd been working on his story for months...	...that every word had been chosen with extreme care. It couldn't be revised, he said.

I sit behind someone in philosophy class who pretends to be taking notes.	But she's actually writing a letter to her friend... I can see it.	Once she even raised her hand and asked a question.	But then she went right back to writing her letter.

Today I sat by the window in a restaurant all morning.

I watched all the people walk by.

It was my roommate Tony's birthday today.

He said he would celebrate like a madman tonight.

I had to stay late at the library to study for a test.

But on my way home I walked by a bar and saw Tony in there.

He was just sitting there, alone.

Tony was his usual self today.

He said none of his friends were available for his birthday party last night.

But all of them promised to do something with him this weekend.

He said he will celebrate like a madman this weekend.

I woke up at 4:30 this morning and couldn't get back to sleep.

So I went outside and walked around.

It was peaceful but strange without all the people.

After a while I went back home and slept till noon.

As I was leaving for the grocery store today, Tony asked me to get him some CoolWhip.

But I forgot to get some.

The strange thing is, Tony never said anything about it.

I guess he forgot too.

Today I showed up an hour early for my philosophy class and read the newspaper.

After a few minutes I'd read everything interesting in it.

So I read beyond the assigned chapters in my philosophy textbook.

It felt good to be ahead in the readings.

My roommate Tony and his friends left for Florida today for spring break.

They're driving an old Volkswagen Bug that sounds like a tractor.

Its headlights are held in place with long strips of duct tape.

"I'd crawl to Florida if I had to," Tony said before he left.

I rode my bike as far out of town as I could today.

No reason, really. It was just something to do.

The countryside was a pleasant change of scenery, and I got a lot of exercise.

I should probably do things like that more often.

Why Jim's Journal?

Readers often ask me why I called this comic strip *Jim's Journal* and not *Scott's Journal*. My name, after all, is Scott.

There are two reasons for that. The first is that *Jim's Journal* sounds a lot better than *Scott's Journal*, because it has that alliteration going for it. The second and more important reason is that the comic strip isn't, and never was, my journal. It's the journal of a comic-strip character.

I had, from the beginning, wanted to make a comic strip that was a little different from other comic strips. One way I thought it could be different was if it used first-person narration instead of straight character dialogue. And I thought the main character of the strip would make a good narrator.

This is a pretty common approach in other media, even in some comic strips, although usually just underground ones. But in the realm of daily newspaper comics, where people are accustomed to seeing only one kind of format (character dialogue only, and on rare occasion some third-party narration—most notably in *The Far Side*), a lot of people were thrown for a loop by *Jim's Journal*. They wondered if this stuff really happened to me, or if Jim was real, or if Jim was my real name, or why on earth a newspaper would print the uneventful journal of this guy named Jim.

I didn't feel like watching TV today.

There was nothing on anyway.

I decided to do some homework instead.

But I didn't feel like doing homework either.

Today in creative-writing class our stories were returned to us, graded.

Mark got a C.

He stayed after class to complain about his grade to the professor.

Later, Mark told me he didn't believe artistic expression should be graded.

My roommate Tony bought a little tape recorder the other day.

He's decided to tape his classes from now on.

Today I went to the music department.

I sat and read a book while listening to people practice their instruments.

Tony has been sitting around watching TV a lot lately—

even more than I usually do, which is quite a bit.

He says it's okay that he's not doing any homework because he has all his classes on tape.

He says he has all weekend to catch up.

Today Mark said he and his friends would be watching a movie on his VCR tonight.

He said the movie would be Dawn of the Dead, his favorite. He said I was invited.

So I went.

Mark & his friends had a lot of the lines memorized and were laughing so much that I couldn't hear the movie.

We had an employee's meeting at McDonald's today.

Everybody was there—even some people I'd never seen before.

Steve, the manager, talked about the good job we've been doing, and how we could improve.

He seemed uncomfortable talking to all those people.

Tony's been taping his classes regularly.

But it seems like he never listens to the tapes—they keep piling up.

Today I borrowed his tape player.

I was going to take a walk and listen to one of my favorite tapes.

But my tape had been erased. It had one of Tony's lectures on it

I stayed up late last night watching TV.

So I was tired today.

In my creative-writing class, Mark was talking to me.

But I was so tired that I wasn't even listening to him.

25

Tony had a big test today. 	He spent most of yesterday catching up on listening to the lectures he taped. 	He told me today that he doesn't think he failed the test. 	He said taping classes is a pretty good idea. 
Tony's parents came to visit for a few days. 	They seemed nice. 	Tony was embarrassed by almost everything they said and did.	"So you're Tony's roommate," they said to me. 
Tony's parents are still here. 	They're staying in a hotel a few blocks away.  But they spend most of their time being shown around the campus by Tony.	Today Tony's dad asked me all about my classes, where I was from, my career plans, and so on. 	But I couldn't think of anything to ask about him. 
Tony's parents left today. 	After he came home from his classes, Tony talked to me for a while. 	He told me all the little things about his parents that bothered him. 	They seemed like okay parents to me. 

26

Today I walked to McDonald's with Ruth, who works there with me.

She told me about her goal of becoming a dental technician.

I made hamburgers, fish fillets and chicken nuggets at McDonald's.

Then I went home.

Today I washed the windows at McDonald's.

I liked it.

I didn't have to pay attention to anything else around me.

I just washed the windows.

Today Mark didn't come to creative-writing class.

The class was quiet without him.

Later in the day I was watching TV while eating some fish sticks.

I wondered why Mark hadn't come to class.

I was sitting around today reading when Tony called.

He said he forgot his notes for an open-notebook test and wanted me to bring them to him.

I said I would.

I wasn't at all inconvenienced by bringing Tony his notes, but he thanked me as if I'd crawled 300 miles to bring them.

For the rest of the day I felt like I'd done a really good deed.

It was a busy day at McDonald's today. (I was making fries.)

When I came home Tony was watching The Brady Bunch on TV.

"Look at those pants Marsha's wearing!" he said, laughing.

It was kind of funny, but I didn't feel like watching the whole show.

I got my phone bill today.

I didn't realize I'd made so many long-distance calls.

From now on I'll write down every long-distance call I make.

And I won't make a long-distance call unless I absolutely have to.

Today I had my Shakespearean drama class.

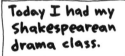

Before class, the person next to me was talking to me.

She said she hated Shakespeare, but is getting a B anyway.

She said she usually gets B's.

Last night I couldn't get to sleep.

The people next door were having a loud party.

This morning I could barely stay awake.

And my roommate Tony told me all about the neighbors' party.

Today at McDonald's I accidentally dropped a tray of hamburgers.

Steve, the manager, didn't say anything about it.

I cleaned up the mess, then continued making hamburgers.

Actually, Steve didn't talk to me all day after I dropped the hamburgers.

I've decided to go back to my home town for the summer.

Today I told Steve, the manager at McDonald's, that I'll be quitting.

He asked if I expected to be rehired after the summer.

I said "not really."

I'd like to work at some place other than McDonald's in the fall.

I studied for my final exams while sitting outside today.

Tony was sitting outside too.

I also saw Sam, from McDonald's.

I told him I'd quit at McDonald's. He said he plans to stay there all summer.

Today I walked by Steve on the sidewalk.

I didn't know he had a baby.

Steve noticed me but he didn't say anything.

I guess I'll probably never see him again.

Summer

I came back to my hometown today.

I talked to my mom for a while.

She wanted to know what I was going to do all summer.

I said I didn't want to do much of anything.

Today my mom left for work in the morning.

(She's a piano teacher.)

I sat around at home.

I read a short story in the Atlantic Monthly today.

(My mom has a subscription.)
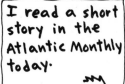

It was okay.

I thought maybe I should write a story, since I didn't have much else to do.

But I didn't really *feel* like it.

My high-school friend Sue came to visit today.

She's home from college for the summer too.

She told me about one of her professors who she said was really eccentric.

She described him and laughed, I could imagine him being pretty funny.

I went for a bike ride today.

I stopped at a gas station and bought a can of Coke.

I sat on the curb and drank it.

It was nice and cold at first, but then it tasted like syrup.

I was bored today.

I went outside and walked around.

I walked by a guy washing his car. A suntan lotion ad was playing on his radio.

When I got home I tried to figure out the notes to the suntan lotion theme on the piano.

Today my high-school friend Dave came over.

He said he and some of our other friends from high school were going to a movie tonight.

He wanted to know if I wanted to come.

I said I would.

I went to a movie last night with Dave and his friends.

Afterwards we went to Hardee's and Gene squashed ketchup packets with his fist.

Dave and the rest of them laughed and people looked at us like we were crazy.

I had an okay time, but I was glad to get home.

I've been sleeping in late all summer.

Today I got up at 1:30.

After a while my mom came home from work.

"Did you just get up?" she said.

She couldn't believe I slept so late.

I went to see my dad today.

He lives just across the state line from my mom.

They got divorced a long time ago.

"Well look who's here," he said.

I rode my bike around today.

I went past my high school.

I walked through it and it looked pretty much the same as I remember it.

There were some guys from the high-school football team training outside.

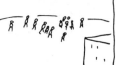

Today I went to visit my friend Sue.

She answered the door and said. "Hi, Jim," then ran back into her house.

I heard her tell me to come in, so I did.

She was watching a soap opera, and told me what was happening on it.

I slept in till 2:00 today.

I ate a bowl of cereal and watched some game shows on TV.

When my mom came home from work I was still sitting around.

"You look like you need something to do," she said.

My mom asked me to mow the lawn today.

It doesn't seem like a big yard, but it took me a long time.

Today one of my high-school teachers came to our house.	She's a friend of my mom. 	She wanted to know all about what I thought of college. 	But I couldn't think of anything to say about it. 
I went to the grocery store today. 	My mom sent me with a list of things to buy. 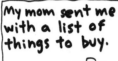	As I was leaving with the groceries, the cashier ran up to me. 	"You forgot your receipt," she said. 
I visited my dad again today. 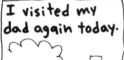	He was painting his garage, and I helped. 	"The old paint was peeling like crazy," he said. 	He told me his neighbors just painted their house and garage. 
My friend Dave came by today. 	He said he was going to another movie tonight with his friends. 	I told him I didn't really feel like coming along. 	He said, "Come on, it'll be a great time!" 

Last night Dave and my other friends stopped by.

They were on their way to a movie.

Dave asked me to come.

I said I felt like staying home.

"You don't want to go out with your ol' high-school pals?" he said.

I guess I just didn't.

When I got up today I saw a note from my mom.

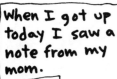

She wanted me to wash a load of clothes.

So I did.

While the washer and dryer were going I looked through my old stuff, which my mom stores in the basement.

Sue came over today.

We sat around and talked.

We agreed that summer can get boring, but it's a nice break from college.

"I can't wait to get out of school and get a job," she said.

(She wants to go into advertising.)

Today I took a walk.

I stopped at Dairy Queen and had a peanut buster parfait.

I sat outside.

I watched an ant, who was walking across the table in a roundabout way.

Fall
Semester

Sophomore
Year

I live in a new apartment with my old roommate Tony, and a new roommate, Steve.

DIKKERS

Tony was angry when he found out that the intercom didn't work.

He got even more angry when he found out that we didn't have a cable TV hookup.

He says our new apartment is a dump, but other than that I think it's an OK place.

This is Tony's and my new roommate, Steve.

Steve went to the same high school Tony did, but was one grade behind Tony.

DIKKERS

Today Tony said Steve doesn't get any space in the refrigerator 'cause he's a freshman.

He was just kidding.

Steve (Tony's and my new roommate) went to the same high school as Tony.

Tony was sitting around today reminiscing about people he remembered from high school.

He was throwing out names and laughing uproariously, asking Steve if he remembered them.

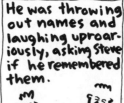

Steve only knew of one or two. I don't think Steve and Tony had the same friends in high school.

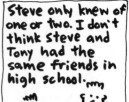

I went to class today.

The person next to me had a new notebook, a new folder, freshly sharpened pencils, and a new 3-ring binder.

She wrote her name, the name of the class, and the name of the professor at the top of a piece of paper.

But she didn't write anything else for the rest of the hour.

I got up early today.

Before class I went to the store to buy some breakfast.

GROCERIE
SALE

Then I went to my first class, which is U.S. history.

Today I was woken up by a loud crunching sound.

There was also the sound of the TV.

Steve was watching Good Morning America and eating Froot Loops right out of the box.

I got up early again today.

I was about to leave for class when Tony woke up.

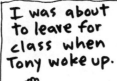

Steve was watching Good Morning America and eating Froot Loops right out of the box.

"How can you eat those without milk?" Tony asked.

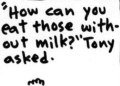

I had my U.S. history class today.

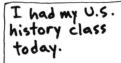

We learned about what life was like in the new-world colonies.

I was taking notes, like I usually do.

The person next to me looked at my notes and wrote everything that I wrote.

Today I went to McDonald's, where I used to work.

I saw a few people I recognized and some that were new.

I talked to Ruth. She said Steve wasn't the manager any more.

The new manager is really nice, and she's looking for people to hire, Ruth said.

Today I went to psychology class.

Then I came home and ate a peanut butter and jelly sandwich.

38

Today Cheryl, the new manager at McDonald's, called me.

She said she'd like me to work at McDonald's.

She sounded pretty desperate.

So I said I would.

On my way home from class today I bought some Pop tarts.

When I got home, Steve and Tony were watching Oprah Winfrey on TV.

I sat and joined them and opened up my Pop tarts.

They both wanted some pop tarts so I gave them some.

I went to my U.S. history class today.

When I came home I felt like reading a little bit of my U.S. history book.

But I realized I had all week-end to read it so I watched TV.

After a while Tony came home, ran into his room, then left in a hurry.

After class today I went to work at McDonald's.

Last time I worked there was 4 or 5 months ago.

I'd forgotten how much hard work it is.

(I worked from 2:30 till 6.)

When I came home from work today I sat and watched TV with steve.

I told him I'd just come back from McDonald's.

He was surprised. He didn't know I worked there.

He said he'd have to come in and eat when I'm working some time.

I ran into Tony on campus today.

He didn't say much except that he needed to borrow a quarter.

I said I didn't have one and he said "Damn it, I'll see ya later, Jim."

I felt pretty bad later when I found a quarter in my pocket.

Mike is a guy who usually works at McDonald's when I'm there.

Today he was squashing old hamburgers in the trash compactor.

He said college can't give you hands-on experience like this.

It was pretty funny.

Cheryl, the manager, thought it was funny too, but she told us to get back to work.

Last night Tony was watching TV with a friend.

I did some homework in my room.

A while later, I went to the kitchen to get a sandwich.

"I'm a pretty sensitive guy," I heard Tony tell his friend.

This morning Tony said "Hey, whadjya think of Karen?"

He was talking about his friend from last night.

I said I didn't meet her or anything, but guessed she was pretty nice.

"'Pretty nice?' She's the hottest chick in town!" he said.

Today Steve was talking to me about Tony's girlfriend.

"Why do you s'pose she likes Tony?" he said.

Then Tony came home... After that we didn't say much.

"Guess who's got a hot date tonight, gentlemen!" Tony said.

After my psychology class today I didn't go home right away.

I wandered around the psychology building and read all the cartoons on the office doors.

Some of them were pretty funny.

They were all cartoons about psychology.

This morning I got up early to study for a U.S. history test.

But I didn't feel like studying, so I watched TV.

After a while, Steve got up and watched TV too.

He asked me if I'd mind turning the channel to Good Morning America.

So I did.

Today Karen came over, looking for Tony.

He wasn't home so she asked me to have him call her.

I left him a note.

It was about 3:30 a.m. when he came home.

He called her, but he didn't make any sense.

This morning I was eating some toast and studying for my U.S. history test.

Then Tony asked me if I remembered what he did last night.

I told him that he gave his friend Karen a call, but that he didn't make much sense.

At first he didn't believe me, then he begged me to remember what he said.

I worked late at McDonald's today.

Mike was there, making jokes about everything.

But I wasn't really in the mood to laugh.

After a while my mouth was tired from pretending to smile, and I just wanted to go home.

Today I was working at McDonald's during lunch.

My roommate Steve came in and said hello.

Then he ordered a Big Mac with no special sauce, no pickles, and double the lettuce.

He also told me not to toast the bun.

Today Tony's friend (who has a car) drove us to the grocery store.

Steve and I sat in the back seat.

Tony sat in front with his friend, laughing, talking and playing tapes.

We spent a lot of money and got a lot of food.

The phone was ringing today when I came home.

Whoever it was hung up before I answered it.

I thought they might call back later.

But the phone didn't ring for the rest of the day.

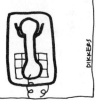

Today I went to my psychology class.

The professor wrote on an overhead projector.

It wasn't focused very well, and I had trouble seeing what she was writing.

All the lights were off too, and I got really sleepy.

Today after my U.S. history class I went to eat a taco.

I read some of my U.S. history textbook while I ate.

It was pretty interesting.

I should probably read my textbooks more often.

Today I didn't feel like getting out of bed.

I don't know why. I just didn't.

Then Tony came into my room and said, "Hey, you bum, get up! There's a phone call for you!"

It was Ruth from McDonald's. She wanted me to work for her today.

I said I would.

Today I went to my psychology class.

Then I went to the store and bought a candy bar.

I guess it's been awhile since I've eaten one.

It didn't taste as good as I remember.

Today was a pretty typical day.

I was sitting around this afternoon watching TV. (So was Steve.)

A police car with its siren going drove by outside.

"They finally caught you, Jim," Steve said.

Today at McDonald's they started an evaluation of the employees.

While I was flipping hamburgers, Cheryl, the manager, watched me.

Today I got a letter from an old high-school friend. 	As I was reading it I felt like writing back.	I thought of all the things I could write about. 	But later, I didn't feel like writing back at all. 
Today my psychology class seemed longer than usual. 	I kept looking at the clock, and it didn't seem to be moving very fast.	When the class finally ended I was really tired. 	So I went home and took a nap. 
Today Steve was sifting through all his belongings. 	"I brought too much stuff when I moved here!" he said. 	I looked through his high-school year book. 	I found his picture and it looked kind of funny. 
Today Steve decided to get rid of the stuff he didn't need. 		He asked me if I wanted his Humphrey Bogart poster. 	I said I didn't. 

Today Steve cleaned his room. 	He vacuumed it and everything. 	When he was done, Tony and I looked at it. 	It was pretty clean. 
I worked until closing time tonight at McDonald's. 	I didn't go home right away. 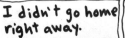	I walked on the train tracks next to the campus. 	It was really quiet, except for cars going by now and then. 
Today Steve came home while I was making a sandwich. 	"I don't think college is for me," he said. 	Then Tony came home and said, "Women! I just can't figure 'em!" 	We sat around in the kitchen and talked about our problems for quite a while. 
I was working at McDonald's today when Tony's girlfriend Karen came in (with a friend). 	"Hey, you're Tony's roommate." she said. 	"Tony...God, what a jerk," her friend said. 	They laughed, even though they were trying not to.  They ordered two ice cream cones.

I was just sit-ting around today when Tony came home.

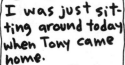

"She never wants to do anything with me anymore, I swear!" he said.

He talked about it for almost an hour, but not really to me.

He made light of it, but I think he was actually pretty sad.

Today Steve rented a movie on video.

It was Star Trek II: The Wrath of Khan.

I didn't really feel like watching it because I had homework to do.

But I ended up watching the whole thing any-way.

We had a test today in my U.S. history class.

Lately I haven't been studying as much as I should.

I had trouble thinking of the answers.

In my psychology class today we had to get in little groups.

We were supposed to think up an undesired behavior.

Nobody in my group knew each other, so it was kind of awkward at first.

Eventually we decided on finger-nail biting.

I went to my U.S. history class today.

I read the assigned chapters in the textbook beforehand.

I felt bad about not studying for the test the other day.

So I decided to try harder this time.

Today at McDonald's we found out the results of our employee evaluations.

Ruth was promoted to crew chief. (She's worked here a long time.)

I got a 10¢-per-hour raise.

So did Mike.

I got up late today to the sound of music I'd never heard before.

It was loud.

Tony was dancing to it in the hall.

He said it was a tape of Eskimo song duels that he had to listen to for his music appreciation class.

Today when I came home from school Tony was watching TV and playing a tape.

I recognized the music. I looked at the tape. It was The Blue Danube.

Tony said he was listening to it for his music appreciation class.

He said it was too boring to listen to by itself, which is why he was watching TV.

"Jim," Tony said today, "if you ever see a record by John Cage, I strongly recommend you don't buy it."

I asked him why he was listening to all this music so late in the semester.

He told me it was because the test wasn't until today.

"I don't know why I ever took this class," he said.

Today I worked at McDonald's flipping hamburgers.

Mike was working on the cash register.

The radio was on and I was getting sick of hearing the same songs over and over.

Once Mike said, "Hey, somebody just ordered a hamburger without the bun!"

Last night Tony and Steve and I watched "How The Grinch Stole Christmas" on TV.

Steve said he always watched shows like The Grinch every Christmas when he was a kid.

Tony said they shouldn't show it on TV so early. "It's November!" he said.

But he said he used to watch it every year too.

There's a 6-page paper due in my psychology class in two days.

Actually, it's an optional paper, but I'd like to do it because it will help my grade.

The trouble is, I can't think of a topic.

49

This is what I looked at almost all day today: a blank sheet of paper

I can't think of a topic for my psychology paper that's due tomorrow.

I actually thought of a topic and wrote 2 pages on it last night.

But it wasn't any good, so I'm back where I started.

I decided not to write that psychology paper.

I told Tony and he said he remembers last year when I worked hard in school.

Now, he said, I'll be lucky if I get a "c" average.

"You'll never get anywhere in life if you don't have good grades," he said.

I'm behind in my classes, so I need to do a lot of work to catch up.

Last night I was doing some homework, but it gave me a headache.

I walked around outside awhile to get some fresh air.

But it didn't help. My head still ached, and I felt even less like doing homework than before.

I went to see a movie last night.

tickets

I came home and told Tony I saw a movie and he said, "You saw a movie all by yourself?!"

Today I went to my psychology class.

When it was over, a guy sitting next to me said, "So, are you ready for the final exam?"

I'd never seen or talked to him before, but he was really friendly.

He said, "I'm not... It's gunna be a couple all-nighters for me," then he laughed.

I didn't have any food today so I went to the grocery store.

Steve said he needed some food too, so he came along.

On the way there, Steve said, "I hate this weather. It's too cold."

Today I went to my psychology class

When I came home, Tony was studying for his finals.

So was Steve.

Today I worked at McDonald's.

Ruth was there.

She said the employees are having a Christmas party and I'm invited.

I said I'd come.

There were a lot of people at the McDonald's Christmas party today, all laughing and talking.

Somebody came up to me and said, "Hi, I'm Wayne, I work mornings."

Cheryl, the manager, talked to me for a while.

I felt awkward talking to her. I'm used to just doing what she says.

I had a final exam today.

I studied for it all last night.

The test had three different essay questions and I had to pick one.

Two of them I didn't know much about, but luckily one of them was pretty easy.

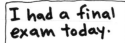

Steve and Tony left for winter break today.

They both live in Hudson, Wisconsin, so they rode there together.

Steve asked me if I could think of anything he could get his parents for Christmas.

"We'll find something on the way there," Tony said. "Let's go!"

It's quiet without Steve and Tony around.

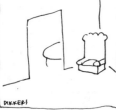

Hardly anybody comes into McDonald's because everybody on campus went home.

My grandma sent me a pair of socks and a Christmas card today.

Spring Semester

Sophomore Year

Panel 1: Today I got some of the books I'll need for my classes.

Panel 2: They cost a lot.

Panel 3: Some of them looked like they'd be fun to read.

Panel 4: But I probably won't want to read them when they're assigned.

Panel 7: Today I had an astronomy class.

Panel 8: The professor used up the whole class reading the syllabus to us.

| Today I had a Chinese history class. 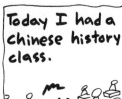 |  |  | Then I came home and read the first few chapters in the text book.  |

| Today I worked at McDonald's.  | During my break, Ruth was telling me what it was like to be crew chief.  | "Being crew chief isn't much different than being one of the crew people," she said.  | She finished her cup of Coke and started chewing on the ice cubes.  |

| Today when I woke up, Tony was leaving for an 8 o'clock class.  | "Top o' the mornin' to ya, Jim," he said.  | He smelled like cologne.  | After he left, I had a bowl of cheerios, and I could still smell the cologne.  |

| My astronomy class made me think today.  | I saw the earth as just a tiny speck floating in space.  | I came home and Steve was watching "Win Lose or Draw."  | I asked him if he ever thought of how insignificant we all are.  He said he has. |

I was bored today.

I flipped around some radio stations for a while...

I went to the bookstore and browsed...

When the day was over, I was amazed at how I'd frittered it away.

I had my Chinese history class today.

I was looking at my desk.

It had political platitudes etched in it...

U.S. out of Central America

#1

Just say NO to Apartheid

and the names of a couple rock bands too.

U2

Guns -N- Roses

Today Tony and I were watching TV and eating.

We heard something get thrown against the wall in Steve's room.

Then Steve stomped out the door and slammed it.

Today I went to a movie with Sam and Ruth, from McDonald's.

Right at the plot climax, the picture went blank, and we just had the sound.

Then they rewound the film and showed the end again, with a picture.

But it wasn't very good because we already had a pretty good idea what happened.

Today after class I ran into Mark. 	He used to work at McDonald's. 	He was in one of my classes last year too. 	He said he hasn't been up to much. 
Today I was going to the grocery store.  (I was all out of cereal.)	I asked Steve if he wanted to come. 	He said he had too much home- work to do. 	But he didn't look like he wanted to do his homework at all. 
At McDonald's today Mike was making fries. 	He accidentally dropped the fry rack and got splattered with boiling grease. 	His arm had dark red spots on it where the grease hit it. 	Cheryl, the manager, put some medication on it. 
Mike came to work today. 	He had a big bandage on his arm from his burn yesterday. 	Once his arm almost touched the Big Mac bun toaster plate (which is really hot). 	We couldn't believe the bad luck of almost getting burned in the same place twice. 

Today Steve and I were just sitting around.

Tony sat down with a plate of spaghettios.

"You know what this place needs?" he said....."A sofa."

"This place definitely needs a sofa," he said.

When I got up today, Tony was looking through the newspaper.

He was pointing out all the ads for furniture.

(He wants to buy a sofa.)

Later, I went to my Chinese History class.

We read Confucius' Analects.

Steve was writing a book report today.

He said it was easy in high school— you just had to write a summary.

"How are you supposed to know how to do a college book report?" he said.

Tony bought a sofa today.

He bought it from his friend Kurt, who helped him move it.

"20 bucks. You can't beat that," Tony said.

After a while we all sat in it and he said, "What do you think, guys?"

I went to the library this morning to read my Chinese history book.

But I didn't feel like reading, so I just doodled in my notebook.

Tony had a couple friends over today.

They were just sitting around talking.

Today I went to my astronomy class.

On my way home I saw Steve.

He had just bought some batteries.

This morning my clock-radio went off, but I didn't feel like getting up.

I listened to the radio for almost an hour.

It was on an all-news station, which had a lot of commercials.

I heard one commercial three times. (It was for Therapeutic Mineral Ice.)

Today I accidentally cut my thumb on a piece of paper.

"Ooh, a paper cut, those are the worst!" Tony said

But it wasn't too bad.

I tried to put on a Band-Aid, but it was hard to open.

The red string just came right out, and I had to tear the little package all up.

Today I got a call from Cheryl, the manager at McDonald's.

She told me I was late for work.

I went there, but I was pretty sure I wasn't supposed to work today.

I looked at the schedule, and it had my name on it for today.

Today Steve came home when Tony and I were sitting around watching TV.

"I've had it. I'm quitting school," he said.

"I'm just not smart enough for college," he said. He was angry.

"Come on," Tony said. "Nobody just up and quits school!"

"What would you do if you quit school?" Tony asked Steve this morning.

"I'll get a job or something," Steve said.

"You're gunna work at McDonald's, like Jim? For the rest of your life?!" Tony said.

"A college degree is your ticket to a decent job," he said.

This morning I was reading the newspaper.

When I was done, Tony took it. "I gotta read my horoscope," he said.

"Damn!" he said.

Today Tony said he was going to the grocery store. 	He asked Steve and me if we needed anything. 	Steve said he could use a box of Froot Loops. 	"Froot Loops?" Tony said. "I'll get something that's good for you." Then he left. 
I was sitting in the kitchen eating some toast this morning. 	Steve came in and said, "Oh no, I'm out of cereal." 	Tony bought him some Cheerios yesterday, but Steve doesn't like Cheerios. 	He got dressed and went to the store. 
Today Steve and I were sitting around watching TV. 	Steve said, "Jim, do you think I should quit school?" 	I said, "I don't know." 	
Today I got up late and skipped my astronomy class. 	Later at night I worked at McDonald's.  Ruth was there.	She had an interview with a dentist today and thought she did pretty well. 	Ruth wants to be a dental technician. 

Today Tony was cleaning the bathroom.

He had his radio on really loud.

I was trying to read my astronomy book, but I couldn't concentrate.

So I listened to the radio.

On my way home from class today I bought a scrub brush.

Tony said we needed one, and asked me if I'd pick one up.

I came home and gave it to him.

"Thanks, Jim," he said. "Now stay out of the kitchen for a while."

(He was cleaning the kitchen.)

I got my bike out today.

I haven't ridden it since September.

Almost everything on it needed to get fixed.

I couldn't figure out how to fix it so I took it to a bike shop.

It should be fixed in a couple days, the guy said.

Steve came back from spring break yesterday.

He brought a kitten with him from his parents' farm.

"I named him Mr. Peterson," Steve said.

Mr. Peterson looked like he was afraid of all of us.

Mr. Peterson, the cat Steve brought home, was hiding in a corner today.

"Come here, Mr. Peterson. Come here, Mr. Peterson," Tony said.

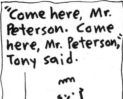

But Mr. Peterson stayed in the corner.

Tony told Steve he should have gotten a dog.

I have to write a paper for my chinese history class.

But I can't think of a topic.

Today I was sitting in the kitchen, eating a bowl of soup.

Steve came in and said, "I'm hungry, but I can't think of anything to eat."

Today Steve and I were watching TV.

"College isn't for me, but I'm going to stick it out for the semester," Steve said.

I asked him what he would do when he left school.

He said he'd go back to his hometown and get a job.

Today in my astronomy class we learned about astrology.

The professor said the Earth's position's changed since ancient times, when astrology started.

So the zodiac signs don't match the constellations they're named after.

He said that's why even if astrology worked, horoscopes would be wrong.

I went to talk to my Chinese-history professor today.

I told him I can't think of a topic for my paper.

He made a lot of suggestions. They all sounded pretty good.

But a little later I still didn't know what to write about.

Today I was eating a peanut-butter and jelly sandwich.

Mr. Peterson looked at me and meowed over and over.

meow meow

It seemed like he really wanted something from me.

meow

But I didn't know what he wanted, so I couldn't help him.

meow meow

I went to my astronomy class today.

Then I came home and ate a tuna sandwich and watched Jeopardy on TV.

Then I worked at McDonald's.

When it was almost closing time, Cheryl said, "It's been a long day."

I still haven't written a Chinese-history paper. I don't have a topic.

Today in class we looked at pictures of pottery from the T'ang Dynasty.

Someone sitting behind me said, "Some of these pots are just outrageous!"

So I decided pottery would be a pretty good topic.

63

This morning I was watching TV and eating some Rice Krispies.

Tony yelled from his room, "Turn that down!"

"I have a test in half an hour and I have to study!" he said.

I was done eating so I just turned the TV off and left for class.

Today I went to the library to look up books on T'ang pottery.

I have to write a paper on it.

I looked at a lot of books.

After a while I got pretty tired and didn't feel like writing the paper anymore.

I went to the library again today.

I'm still looking through books to research my term paper.

I felt like going home and taking a nap.

One time I looked at a page in my book and saw the words as just a big gray blob.

I finished my Chinese-history paper over the weekend.

It turned out okay. I hope I never have to write another one.

Today Tony said, "Hey, Jim, think of a topic for my poli-sci term paper."

I told him I didn't want to think about term papers anymore.

Ruth was working at McDonald's today.

She was talking to me about the weather.

She said she likes winter because she grew up in the North.

But she said she's happy that it's warming up.

I accidentally left my jacket at McDonald's yesterday.

Ruth brought it to me on her way home from work today.

"She's huge!" Tony said.

Today Steve said, "Jim, did you ever read The Prince by Machiavelli?"

I told him I was pretty sure I had.

"It's pretty interesting," he said.

"Is that a tuna sandwich?" he asked. I said it was.

Today Tony, Steve and I watched The Music Man on TV.

Tony said his high school put on the play and he had two or three lines.

He was waiting to see the part he played.

Finally he said, "There! that was me!" And he tried to say the lines along with the scene.

Today at McDonald's Mike and I had to clean the walk-in refrigerator. 	We took all the boxes of ketchup, shake mix and stuff down stairs. It took a long time. 	After a while Mike stopped. He was breathing hard. 	"I don't think this is my calling, Jim." he said. 
Tony and I were watching TV Today. 	Tony was eating a couple hot dogs, and Mr. Peterson wanted some. 	"Doesn't Steve ever feed his cat?" Tony said. 	I said I was pretty sure Steve fed him. 
Today Steve came home from school with a test he got back, graded. 	He said he got a D. 	"You passed!" Tony said. "Good goin'!" 	Steve said he's been trying really hard. "I don't know why I bother," he said.
Tony was studying for a test today. 	"I'll never learn all this by tomorrow!" he said.	Then Steve told Tony that cramming isn't the best way to study. 	"Look who's talking," Tony said, "Albert Einstein in the flesh." 

Mr. Peterson woke me up today. 	He was sitting on me kneading his paws. 	I got up and noticed Steve and Tony were gone, and Mr. Peterson's food bowl was empty. 	I put some food in it and he ate it. 
Today at McDonald's Ruth was telling me about her job interview. 	She said she wants to be a dental assistant but didn't get the job. 	"There are a lot of dentists," she said. 	"But you'd be surprised how hard it is to find openings for dental assistants," she said. 
Today I went to my astronomy class. 	Then I came home and ate a sandwich and watched some game shows. 	Steve watched for a while too. 	He guessed at the answers to the game shows' questions. 
I tried to do some homework today. 	But I didn't feel like it, so I took a walk outside. 	I went to an ice cream store and bought a chocolate shake. 	When I finally got home it was time for me to go to work at McDonald's. 

Tony called his dad today.

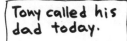

"Leave me alone! This is a private conversation," he said.

His dad had a big operation and just got out of the hospital.

When Tony was done and sat by Steve and me, Mr. Peterson ran away really fast.

Today I heard Tony from the next room, "Jim, you gotta see this!"

When I looked, Mr. Peterson ran away really fast.

"You scared him!" Tony said.

Tony explained how Mr. Peterson was playing with Tony's shoelaces.

Today Tony got some barbecue mix to make a barbecue burger.

The mix made too much so he gave Steve and me some burgers.

When we were done eating, Tony said, "I cooked, so you guys get to do the dishes."

The bowl Tony used had a big orange stain in it that wouldn't come off.

Today in my Chinese history class we got our term papers back.

I got a C-.

I used to get higher grades by not working very hard.

I guess classes are getting harder.

A few days ago Tony won some movie tickets from a radio contest.

Today he said, "Hey, let's all go! This is our last week of school, let's celebrate!"

We went to the movie and it was pretty bad.

While we were walking home Tony said he didn't think it was that bad.

Today was the last day of classes for the semester.

It was a warm day and everybody wanted to be outside.

The professor ended class a little early and said, "Have a good summer."

Everybody put their books away and left in a hurry.

I went out looking for a job today.

Tony said I should stuff envelopes on my own time at home. "That's what I'm doing!" he said.

I went to a movie theater and the manager said they didn't need anybody.

But he gave me an application anyway and said he'd put it on file.

Yesterday I applied for jobs at a copy shop, a book store, a clothing store, a futon store, a movie theater, a newspaper and a bank.

Today I took all the applications back.

Most people said they'd call me and let me know.

It didn't seem like anybody would hire me, but I'm sure I'll get a job somewhere.

I Got a Job and it wasn't that bad

Now we're into the comics that made up the second Jim collection, *I Got a Job and it wasn't that bad.*

My first job was at McDonald's. I worked there for about eight months, and I liked it. It was a good first job.

I put Jim to work at McDonald's because I remembered enough about my experience there that I could create a realistic backdrop for him.

When I was tired of Jim being at McDonald's, I put him to work in a bookstore, which was my second major job. I worked at the college bookstore at the University of Bridgeport. I met a lot of great people there. Jean, the manager at the bookstore where Jim works, was directly inspired by Martha, the manager at the Bridgeport store where I worked.

I also had a really good experience learning everything about working in a bookstore. Incidentally, that experience helped me greatly when I self-published my first book of Jim cartoons and had to deal with a lot of different bookstore buyers.

Anyway, Jim's work life mirrored my own directly, at least in the beginning.

My next major job after working at the bookstore was drawing a daily comic strip, namely *Jim's Journal.* This posed a problem. I didn't want Jim to be a cartoonist, especially not the cartoonist of a cartoon about a character who draws a cartoon—that's too many layers of self-reference. Also, I wanted Jim to keep working minimum-wage jobs, because his life had to remain uneventful in order for the strip to work, and cartooning might seem too interesting to some. So I got him a job at a copy store. I had never worked in one, but I was spending enough time at Kinko's and other places making copies of *Jim's Journal* cartoons to send out to newspapers that I figured I knew enough about working in a copy shop to fake my way through the details. Also, I figured the constant drone of all those machines at the copy store would make Jim—as they did me—feel characteristically unengaged.

Later, Jim would get a job at a grocery store. I've never worked at one, but my friend Jay Rath, who helped me write and pencil *Jim's Journal* in the later years, worked—and still works—at a grocery store.

I bought a newspaper today. 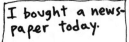	I read it while I ate some toasted bagels. 	When I finished eating, I sat there for a while and read some more. 	Tony walked by, flipped through the paper and took the sports section and entertainment section. 
Today I was sitting at my desk, reading. 	Every once in a while Mr. Peterson would run by my door really fast, playing. 	Once he stopped right in front of it and looked at me with his eyes wide open. 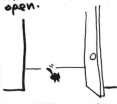	Then he took off running as fast as he could. 
Tony flipped his calendar to March yesterday.	It's the Sports Illustrated swimsuit calendar. He got it for Christmas.	"I love it," he said today. "But I get sick of seeing the same girl all month."	"If they had a different girl for every day," he said, "that'd be something."
Today I was just sitting around watching TV. (Bewitched was on.) 	Kurt, Tony's friend, came over. He was eating a bag of cheese puffs. 	Tony wasn't around so Kurt came in and waited for him. 	He sat and watched Bewitched with me and laughed out loud. 

Today Tony said we needed a shelf for our apartment. 	So he, Steve and I drove to a furniture store and bought one. 	Tony tied the trunk on top of it and said, "That ain't goin' nowhere!" 	When we first got it home Tony couldn't find a place for it. 
Steve got the mail today. 	He walked up to me, flipping through the letters. 	"Nothing for you, Jim," he said. 	"I guess nobody likes you," he said. 
I found a dime on the sidewalk today. 	Even though a dime isn't worth much, I felt pretty good about finding it. 	After walking a ways farther, I almost thought I saw another dime. 	But it was just a little round metal thing. 
Ruth stopped by to visit me today. 	We got talking about when we used to work at McDonald's. 	We laughed pretty hard, remembering the good times and the funny things we did. 	Ruth tried to stop laughing and delicately cleared her throat. 

I was sitting at my desk today trying to read.

But I didn't really feel like reading.

I accidentally flicked a tiny piece of notebook paper fringe on the floor and Mr. Peterson jumped on it.

I flicked more fringes and Mr. Peterson jumped on all of them.

Today I was sitting around nibbling on some potato chips.

Steve was making himself some lunch and singing "Tutti-frutti."

The whole apartment was pretty quiet except for Steve's slightly out-of-tune singing.

After a few minutes, Tony yelled from the other room, "Will you shut up!"

Yesterday I was thirsty for some orange juice, so I went to the store to buy some.

I looked at all the tabloids while I waited in line.

Today Steve said, "Hey, Jim, can I have some of your orange juice?" I said yes.

Then Tony came by and said, "Hey-OJ! Can I have some? I said yes.

I got a call from the bookstore today.

(I applied for a job there the other day.)

I'm supposed to go in for an interview tomorrow.

I felt pretty good about it, but Tony says jobs are for proles.

I went to the bookstore today to interview for a job.

I talked to Jean, the manager, who had a bunch of keys hanging from her belt.

She told me about the job and said I could start tomorrow if I was interested.

Then she asked me where I was from and that kind of thing.

I told Steve and Tony I got a job at the bookstore.

"That's fantastic!" Tony said. "You can buy books for us with the company discount!"

He made a list of all the books he wanted.

Steve said he was planning to get the Cliffs Notes for Great Expectations and asked if we had it in stock.

I said I didn't know.

Today was my first day on the job at the bookstore.

A guy named Paul taught me shipping and receiving.

"You find the packing slip, then you fill out one of these forms and file it under the publisher."

That was all he said.

I wasn't really sure what I was supposed to do.

Last night I was washing my face in the sink.

When I was done I didn't feel like moving or drying my face off.

I just let the water drip off my face for a while.

I went to work at the bookstore today.

Nobody ever really explained what I was supposed to do when I started shipping & receiving the other day.

Jean, the manager, seems pretty nice, so I asked her what I was supposed to be doing.

"Shipping and receiving!" she said.

I got up a little late today.

I wanted a bowl of cereal but we were out of milk.

I went to the corner store to buy some more.

When I came back I ate my bowl of cereal and gave Mr. Peterson some milk too.

Today Tony was watching Jeopardy and eating some hot dogs.

Mr. Peterson was standing on his hind legs in front of Tony.

He put some ketchup on his finger and Mr. Peterson licked it off.

"Hey," Tony yelled, "Mr. Peterson likes ketchup. I can't believe this crazy cat."

When my alarm went off this morning I didn't feel like getting up at all.

I laid in bed while my clock-radio played Your Kiss Is on My List, by Hall and Oates.

I was too lazy to get up and turn it off.

That song stuck in my head for the whole day.

The bulb in my lamp burned out today so I bought a new one.

I went to the hardware store.

I found the bulb, brought it to the register, and the man said, "So, will this be all for you today?"

I said yes, and he rang it up.

beep beep

Today I was just sitting around in my room.

Tony came in and said, "Hey, what's the word for being innocent in a trial?"

"Why can't I think of it? It's right on the tip of my tongue," he said.

I couldn't think of it either.

We couldn't believe neither of us could think of it. Finally I realized it was acquitted.

At the bookstore today I started getting the hang of shipping and receiving.

Paul, the guy who trained me, was there.

He didn't say much. He looked kind of tired.

Once he grunted and said, "This is a hell hole."

Today I was just sitting around watching TV.

A really old movie was on. Cary Grant was in it.

Tony watched it for a while too.

We laughed at some parts of it.

Tony asked me how I liked working at the bookstore and I said it was okay.

Today at the bookstore Jean came down to shipping & receiving, where I work.

I asked her why Paul is always so grumpy.

She said Paul is only like that when he's down here.

She said after a while I'll get to work upstairs and I'll realize how rotten shipping and receiving is.

Today Tony and I were watching TV when it broke all of a sudden.

The sound was still there, but the picture was completely fuzzy.

Tony tried to fix it, but he couldn't.

He hit the side of it then looked at it for a few seconds. "That usually works," he said.

Today I went to the store to buy some cottage cheese and a pear.

On my way home I saw the newspaper in one of those dispensers.

It looked like it might be kind of interesting, so I bought one.

I went home and ate my pear and cottage cheese and read the newspaper.

Today at the bookstore we unloaded boxes of books from a delivery truck.

Jean looked inside and noticed that the books weren't the ones she ordered.

She was angry, and talked to the driver, then called the distributor.

I took the long way home from work.

It was a pleasant walk.

Today Steve rented Robocop and we all watched it.

It was pretty good.

Afterwards, I made myself a tuna sandwich.

Mr. Peterson kept jumping up on the counter even though I kept setting him back on the floor.

I had a hard time getting up today.

My alarm went off at 7, but I reset it for 7:30.

At 7:30 I reset it for 8, and at 8 I reset it for 8:30.

I thought I'd feel more like getting up each time, but I never did.

Today I was just sitting around when the phone rang.

It was somebody who wanted to ask me some questions for a marketing survey.

I answered her questions even though they didn't seem very important.

When she was done she thanked me as if I'd done a great deed.

Today Steve said he's going to some friends' house to watch videos tonight.

"They rented all the Halloween sequals. Wanna come?"

I said I'd rather stay home.

Tony and his friends planned a night out too.

One of his friends was wearing a Pat Sajak mask.

They said they'd raise some hell tonight.

This morning I was eating a bowl of cereal.

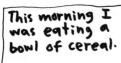

Then Steve got up and ate a bowl of cereal too.

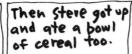

Then Tony sat down and ate sweet tarts and tootsie rolls.

"I got these last night," he said. "We went out trick-or-treating and actually got some candy!"

At work today I stocked shelves.

Jean taught me how to do it the other day.

I feel like I'm getting to know this job better.

Once, somebody asked me where the history section was—and I knew.

Today I was walking down the sidewalk.

An ambulance drove by and its siren was so loud it hurt my ears.

Then I started thinking how strange the cracks in the sidewalk would be if you were really small.

They'd be like giant trenches with rocks and other residue collected in there.

Today I was taking out the garbage to the dumpster behind our building.

Tony came running after me saying, "Jim, wait! Don't throw that away!"

He rummaged through the bag.

"Ah ha! There it is!" he said, holding up half a piece of paper with some writing on it.

Today Steve asked Tony and me if we wanted a part in a movie.

He has to make one for a film class he's taking.

Tony said, "why not? I think I could act pretty good."

Steve told Tony he'd have to act like a real jerk for the part he had in mind.

Steve started filming his movie today.

I helped.

We filmed on the sidewalk just outside our apartment building.

Tony had to walk down the sidewalk and throw litter in the grass.

Steve had him do it two or three times and Tony said, "This is boring. C'mon, let's get moving."

Today Tony asked Steve what his movie was going to be about.

Steve said it was going to be kind of experimental.

Tony said, "It's not gonna suck is it?"

Steve said, "I hope not," and chuckled.

Steve finished filming his movie today.

Tony had to kill himself with a piece of glass.

Steve wanted to put ketchup all over Tony's shirt.

They got into a big argument because Tony wanted to put on a different shirt and Steve said he couldn't because it wouldn't make any sense in the movie.

We were all just sitting around watching TV today.

Mr. Peterson ran past us as fast as he could.

He went into another room and meowed over and over.

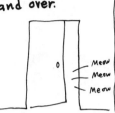

Meow
Meow
Meow

We went in there and couldn't figure out what all the fuss was about—he was just sitting there.

Today Steve showed Tony and me the movie he made.

It was fun to see all the shots we filmed all put together. And he had music for it too—the Peter Gunn theme.

Tony kept saying, "This isn't bad, I'm a pretty good actor."

Steve told us he got a C and we couldn't believe it.

I bought a book today—Anthem, by Ayn Rand.

I decided I needed something to read.

It's really short, so it shouldn't take me too long to read, I figured.

I meant to read a little bit before I went to sleep, but I stayed up till 3 a.m. and read the whole thing.

Steve came home today eating some of that long stick candy that you lick and dip into flavored powder.

"I haven't had this stuff since I was a kid," he said.

Tony said, "How can you even think of eating that crap?"

"It's just sugar is all it is!" he said.

Today when I got up Tony was watching CNN News.

He told me he wanted to keep up with current events more.

"It's important to know what's going on in the world," he said.

At work today I put little magazine subscription flyers inside new books.

I've been learning to run the cash register at the bookstore.

It was pretty busy today.

I told one guy that his text-books would cost $140.

He got out his checkbook and said, "If money is all you love, then that's what you'll receive."

Today I walked by a newspaper recycling bin and noticed a plastic cup in it.

I thought to myself that the cup shouldn't be in there.

But I didn't take it out and throw it in the trash can.

I figured somebody else would probably sort it out eventually.

Last night Tony said he was going to a big party.

"Don't wait up for me!" he told Steve and me.

He came home late, drinking a beer. "This is only my third," he said, "and it hasn't even affected me."

"It's like the situation in China," he said.

Then he made an analogy between the two things in a babbling sort of way.

Today while I was taking a shower the water suddenly scalded me twice.	Tony took a shower after I did.	After he was in there a while he suddenly yelled, "Ouch! Geez, what's going on here?"	About a minute later he yelled, "Aaaah!! Damn this water!"

   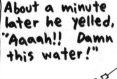 

Today Tony and I were sitting around watching TV.	Tony was flipping around the channels with the remote control.	Steve came up and said we should ask our landlord to fix our scalding shower.	Tony said, "Yeah, I'll give that bum a piece of my mind." But we all forgot to call him.

Today Tony visited the people who live next door to us.	He figured out that our shower turns scalding hot whenever they flush their toilet. 	He called our landlord and told him to fix it. 	When he hung up, he said, "It's as easy as that. He said he'd fix it tomorrow." 
While Tony was taking a shower this morning, he swore like crazy, over and over. 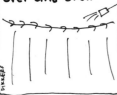	Steve and I avoided him for a while afterwards.	He called our landlord and said, "Hey, would you fix our shower? You said you'd fix it last week!"	When he hung up, he said, "What a bum." 
Today a maintenance man from the landlord's company fixed our shower. 	(It was scalding us whenever the neighbors flushed their toilet.) 	Mr. Peterson sniffed the man's shoes while he was working, then ran away whenever the man moved. 	When the man was done, he said, "That oughta do it for ya." 
Today Rick and I were loading books into upstairs storage. 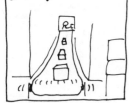	We had fun riding up the conveyor belt and making jokes. 	He told me he had a crush on his roommate. 	I don't know why he told me. It didn't really fit in the conversation.  I guess he just needed to tell somebody.

Steve got the mail today.

He gave me mine and said, "Hey, Jim, you may have already won two million dollars."

Then Steve and Tony made fun of me, thinking of how I'd spend two million dollars.

I watched the crumbs of my peanut butter and jelly sandwich fall onto my plate.

Today I got up early and was really tired.

I got out of bed thinking I might be able to wake up.

But I was too tired, so I decided to go back to sleep.

But Mr. Peterson was lying on my pillow.

At the bookstore for the past few weeks Jean's had us reorganizing downstairs storage.

Rick and I were supposed to be down there today sorting stuff.

But we hardly did any work, and mostly just talked and joked around.

And Jean was too busy running the store upstairs, so she never checked up on us.

Today Ruth, Steve and I went to eat at Wendy's.

Steve was telling us how much he couldn't wait to get out of school.

"I loved school," Ruth said. "I wish I could go back."

Steve couldn't believe Ruth liked school, and said, "You can take my place then."

I was watching TV and eating a hot dog today when the phone rang.

Tony answered it and said, "Jim's busy watching Green Acres, can I take a message?"

But he was just kidding, and handed me the phone.

It was Jean, from the bookstore. She wanted to know if I could work Saturdays.

I told her I could.

Today at the bookstore Rick and I had to price 25 boxes of new books and put them on the shelf.

We figured out the price from the invoice, which we're supposed to do, then put stickers on.

But Jean saw the books and said the prices were wrong. We used wholesale instead of retail prices.

We had to peel off all the stickers and put new ones on.

Today Tony and I were watching TV.

The NBC Nightly News was on.

"I'm gonna get so sloshed tonight," Tony said.

At the bookstore today I was shelving self-help books.

There was dust and crumpled-up gum wrappers way back behind the books.

Rick, who was working with me, walked by and said, "Those shelves could use some dusting, but don't tell Jean!"

I decided Rick was probably right.

I went to the grocery store today.

I wanted to buy some oranges. But they had a bad selection.

They all had bruised or molded spots, and were displayed so you couldn't see the spots.

But I managed to find a couple good oranges.

At the bookstore today I was punching in on the time clock.

I noticed Jean laughing and trying to run away from Rick.

Jean had a secret about Rick and was going to tell everybody.

I didn't know what it was all about, but everybody was having a good time—even Rick.

Today Steve said he was going to get Mr. Peterson fixed.

"That's mean," Tony said. "You should let him sow his wild oats first."

Steve told Tony that everybody he talked to said it's best to fix cats early.

I looked at Mr. Peterson and it almost seemed like he knew his fate was being discussed.

Steve took Mr. Peterson to the vet today to get neutered.

Mr. Peterson has been to the vet before, and doesn't like it.

When Steve came back he said, "Hey, guess what. Mr. Peterson's a girl."

Tony was watching TV, and he mumbled, "Big deal, a cat's a cat."

Today Steve brought Mr. Peterson back from the vet.

She had a little square bald spot on her stomach, and looked tired.

Today at the bookstore I worked the cash register.

Jean, the manager, came up to me and said, "How's it goin', Jim?"

I said I was fine, and told her about Mr. Peterson getting fixed.

She said, "You remind me of my little brother."

When I came home from work today Mr. Peterson was sitting on the couch.

She looked at me while I came in and took off my coat.

I sat next to her for a while and scratched her head, but she didn't purr like usual.

Then I got up and made a tuna sandwich.

I worked at the bookstore again today.

Somebody was sick and Jean called me in to work.

I was doing invoicing when Jean came up to me.

"The shelves in the self-help section are filthy," she said. "Jim, why don't you dust those shelves when you're done here."

I got up around 8:30 today.

I noticed Tony sleeping in his clothes on the couch.

I took a shower, poured a bowl of cereal, and a lot of other noisy things.

And Tony didn't wake up— he didn't even turn over.

I did a load of laundry today.

I got the washing machine started and went back to my room.

When I came back, the clothes were all covered with grains of soap, even though the machine was done.

I figured that machine was broken, so I washed my clothes in a different one and they came out fine.

Today I worked on the cash register at the bookstore.

Hardly any people came in to buy anything.

So I just sat there and didn't have to work very hard.

Today I was sitting around petting Mr. Peterson.

I scratched up and down her back and she purred like crazy then fell asleep on my lap.

After a few minutes, the phone rang, so I had to get up and answer it.

I lifted her up and set her down on the chair, and she stayed in the exact same position she was in on my lap.

Today I took a walk around town.

I went to an art gallery and looked at the art.

It was nice to get away from everything for a while.

Today when I got up I was really tired.

I set my alarm for an hour later and went back to sleep.

When I got up again, I was still really tired.

When I got up and saw Steve, he said, "Rise and shine, Jim!" and that made me feel like going back to sleep again.

Today Tony was listening to a top-40 radio station.

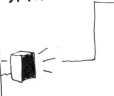

He was cleaning up some of his stuff around the apartment, singing along with the music.

Then some commercials came on—the kind with music in them.

And Tony sang along with those too.

Today I was reading a book at the cash register at the bookstore.

Jean told me to put the book away so I could watch what I was doing.

But nobody was in the store, so there was nothing to watch.

Today I bumped into Dean, a guy I sort of knew in college.

We talked for just a couple minutes about school, and he joked about his coat, which he got for christmas.

We came to a corner and he said, "I go this way, see you around, Jim."

I walked aways more and for a brief second I couldn't remember who I'd bumped into.

I was in the kitchen washing dishes today while Tony was eating a pot pie.

Once, he looked up like he was deep in thought.

He said, "I've decided something: paper towels are a complete waste."

"Why waste money on paper towels when you can wash a real towel as much as you want and use it over and over?" he said.

Today at the bookstore Jean said, "Jim, would you come see me when your shift's over with?"...I worked for 5½ hours and that whole time tried to imagine what she might have to say.

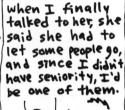

When I finally talked to her, she said she had to let some people go, and since I didn't have seniority, I'd be one of them.

She said she was sorry and wished she didn't have to do it.

While I walked home, the traffic, people, and all the other noises seemed a lot more vivid than usual.

Today I was wandering around the apartment when no one else was around.

Mr. Peterson followed me around.

I went into Tony's room and looked at all the bumper stickers on his trash can.

I went into Steve's room and everything was neat and clean.

Tony went to the dentist today.

He said he hadn't been to the dentist for a long time. "And it wasn't that bad," he said.

He said they gave him a toothbrush and some dental floss.

Steve and I realized we hadn't gone to the dentist in a long time either.

Last night I was bored, so I turned on the radio and flipped around the stations.

I found some relaxing music and just sat there and listened to it for a long time.

I called to make an appointment with a dentist today.

They said they had an opening tomorrow.

Also today I sat outside for a while and looked at the sidewalk.

I had my dentist appointment today.

I sat in the waiting room for a few minutes and read People magazine.

The dentist used rubber gloves when he cleaned and checked my teeth, and I could taste and smell the rubber.

My teeth felt smooth and clean when I left.

Today I noticed Mr. Peterson clawing up the stereo speakers.

scratch
scratch
scratch

Tony saw her too, and said, "Shoo! Shoo! Those are expensive speakers, you goofy little varmint!"

Steve told Tony that the speaker covers are only decorative, and clawing didn't damage the speakers at all.

"Maybe you'd feel different if they were _your_ speakers." Tony said.

(They're Tony's.)

I took Mr. Peterson outside today.

We just sat on the steps outside our building.

Mr. Peterson was really tense and darted her head around at every little sound.

When I tried to take her back inside, she sniffed my hand like she didn't know who I was.

Today Steve bought a leash for Mr. Peterson so he can take her outside.

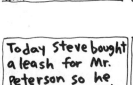

"It's spring after all," Steve said.

He put the leash on her and she flipped around trying to get it off.

Tony and Steve laughed like crazy.

When I got out of the shower this morning I realized my towel wasn't there.

I thought I might have left it in my room because I was going to do some laundry.

I used Tony's towel to dry myself off.

It smelled like Tony.

Steve and Ruth and I rented a movie last night and ate popcorn out of a big bowl.

Mr. Peterson kept sitting up to look inside the bowl.

"Look out Mr. Peterson, you'll tip over the bowl," Ruth kept saying.

Mr. Peterson kept sitting up to look, but never tipped over the bowl.

Today I was walking into our apt. building when I saw Tony sunbathing in the lawn.

He was playing some rap music on his radio.

"You ought to come out here, man, the sun is great," he said.

When I said I didn't feel like it, he said, "I swear you'd make a great hermit, Jim."

Last night I wasn't tired enough to get to sleep.

I sat in bed and let my mind wander.

I got thinking about being locked in a dungeon in a castle and how I'd escape.

I don't know what I thought about after that. I must have fallen asleep.

I moved into my own apartment today.

(Steve, Tony and I decided to get different apartments a few months ago.)

(Tony is living in the same building as me only down the hall.)

My new place is really small.

I was sitting in the kitchen today eating a sandwich.

Mr. Peterson was sitting by the door, meowing.

meow
meow

I let her out in the hall for a while.

After she got over being scared of it, she ran up and down the hall really fast.

I watched a street juggler today for a while.

when he was done he juggled five balls and flipped his hat out for a finish.

Then he asked everybody to put money in the hat.

Most people walked away. He looked right at me and I felt guilty so I gave him some money.

I saw Tony today.

He'd just gotten his mail.

He was pretty happy about something. He said, "Hey ho, Jim."

He shook an envelope in my face and laughed, "He he he hee!"

"It had a big check in it," he said.

Today I went to the library and checked out a book.

It was Cider House Rules. I figured it'd be a pretty good book to read.

When I was walking into my apartment, a guy said. "How are you today?"

I told him I was fine.

Ruth and I rented an old black-and-white Flash Gordon movie today.

Ruth said she normally doesn't care for science fiction, but thought this was pretty good.

Today I slept in really late because I didn't feel like getting up.

Mr. Peterson was sleeping on the floor in a spot where the sun was shining through.

I wanted to eat something but I didn't have enough energy to make anything.

Then I watched TV.

My mom called today.

She said she was going on a trip to San Francisco

(for a piano-teaching conference).

She said she was really excited about going and said she'd send me a postcard.

Today I called Steve to see if he wanted to do something.	He came over and we just sat around. 	His tennis shoes were stark white. 	I asked him if he got new shoes and he said yes. 
I've been reading Cider House Rules. It's a pretty good book. 	Today when I was reading it, Mr. Peterson jumped up on my lap.	She sat right on the book, so I couldn't read it. 	
Today I walked by a movie theater. 	It was the early afternoon, so they were closed. 	I looked inside and it was completely dark. 	I looked at the movie poster outside—it had creases in it from being folded. 
Today when I was opening the door to my apartment, I saw this guy from a few doors down. 	He was walking very briskly. 	"Hey, how's it goin'?" he said. 	I told him everything was going fine. 

| Today I was walking around outside.  | I was waiting to cross a busy street when I noticed a particular car go by.  | It had a bunch of people in it waving wildly at me.  | But I didn't recognize them or anything.  |

| Today I was tired so I took a nap. It was around 3 p.m.  | When I got up it was dark outside. I couldn't believe I slept so long. | I watched TV and noticed everything was running late.  | It was because of a presidential address or something.  |

| Today my phone rang and I answered it.  | Nobody was there, so I hung up.  | It rang again, and nobody was there again, so I hung up.  | The third time it started ringing I just let it ring, and it rang a million times. |

| Steve and I were sitting around watching TV today.  | There was a commercial on for a car or something.  | Steve said, "Yeah, right," in response to one of the claims the ad made.  | "Commercials are just the dumbest things," he said.  |

I went to a park today, sat on a bench and tossed popcorn to the ducks.

It was fun watching them.

One duck was afraid of the popcorn and wouldn't go near it.

Another duck loved the popcorn. He was really small, but would challenge ducks twice his size to get at each kernel.

Today Ruth told me she was going to visit her parents for a few days.

"I really miss seeing my family," she said.

Then she said, "Jim, you should come with me! It would be really fun!"

So I said I would.

I stopped by Tony's apartment today.

He asked me how everything was going and offered me a can of soda.

The soda company had an instant-win game on the can.

Be an Instant Winner! $ $ $ $

Tony said if my can turned out to be a winner, he'd get to claim the money because he bought the soda.

I went out for a walk today.

I walked quite a ways, but never got tired or felt like stopping.

It seemed like the more I walked, the more invigorated I got

I bet I walked for three hours.

Today Steve brought a couple of friends over.

One of them saw Mr. Peterson and said, "Oh, look, a kitty! She's so cute!"

They stayed around a few minutes, then left.

After they left, Mr. Peterson sat by the door like she wanted to go out too.

Today Ruth picked me up to go to her parents' house

(She invited me to come along with her the other day.)

She said, "I really like this little car," but kept talking about things like the radio not sounding very good and the gas gauge not working.

We drove for almost five hours.

Last night Ruth and I arrived at her parents' house.

Ruth's mom met us at the door and said, "Is this the friend you brought along?"

Ruth's parents started asking us how our trip was, and Ruth's dad was mostly watching the news on TV.

Today Ruth and her mom made everybody breakfast. Ruth's sister was telling me she could play the clarinet.

Today Ruth and I left her parents' house.

Ruth's mom said, "It was fun having you, Jim. Come back and visit any time."

Once we got on the road, Ruth talked about her family and her dog.

She also said she picked up some tapes from her house so we could listen to them in the car.

Today I did some laundry.

I walked down to the basement where the washing machines are.

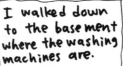

In the stairway I passed the guy who lives down the hall from me.

"Doin' some laundry?" he said.

I watched a game show today.

Contestants had to guess the meanings of made-up personalized license plates.

I also finished reading Cider House Rules today.

It was a pretty good book.

Today I went to a diner.

I ate an order of fries and read a newspaper.

The diner had a lot of odd things hanging on the wall.

There was a giant airplane propeller and also a page from a children's book that they framed.

Today when I got up my throat was sore—it felt like it was closed up.

When I talked, it sounded like I was squawking.

Tony said, "What's the matter, Jim? You entering puberty?"

My throat got less sore as the day wore on.

I stayed home today and wrapped myself in a blanket and watched TV.

I hardly ever got hungry, and when I did I only ate soup.

There are some really dumb TV shows on in the day time.

I stood and stared in the mirror today.

I got really close and looked at the tiny patterns in the iris part of my eye.

Mr. Peterson was walking around the sink, which is right under the mirror.

I lifted her up to show her herself in the mirror, but she didn't seem to be interested in it.

Steve and I were walking by a copy store today.

There was a "help wanted" sign in the window, and Steve said he should apply.

We went in to get an application and I decided to fill one out, too.

I wrote down my experience at McDonald's and the book store, but couldn't remember the exact dates I worked there.

I got a postcard from my mom today.

It was from San Francisco, where she went for a piano teachers conference.

She said she was having a great time riding trolleys, seeing the Golden Gate Bridge and stuff.

I couldn't read it in the top right-hand corner because the postmark covered up her writing.

Today Tony told me he needed to write a resumé.

He showed me a book he bought on how to write a resumé.

He also got resumés from some friends to use as guides.

"I'm ready to go!" he said.

Then he asked me if I knew how to write a resumé.

Tony bought a new tape today, and he was listening to it while he worked on his resumé.

(It was a Fine Young Cannibals tape.)

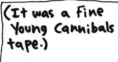

Today I got a call from the manager of the copy store.

He said he wanted me to come down for an interview.

(I applied for a job there the other day with Steve.)

I went there and met the manager. His name was Hal.

Today I told Steve I got a job at the copy store.

He said it was no fair that we both applied and only I got the job.

Then Tony said, "Steve, why would you even want a peon job like that? You need to start thinking management."

"My brother," Tony said, "is manager of a shoe store and makes more money than all of us!"

103

I was sitting around today not doing much of anything when I heard somebody pounding on my window.

It was Tony, and I heard him yell through the glass, "Could you let me in the building— I lost my keys!"

I went out and opened the door for him.

"It's been a doozie of a day, Jim," he said.

I went to work at the copy store today.

Hal, the manager, showed me how to run a big copy machine and got me started making 3,000 copies of something.

After about 3 minutes, the machine got jammed.

I went looking for Hal so he could show me how to fix it, then a customer told me her machine was jammed and asked me to fix it.

I worked at the copy store again today.

I was making 200 copies of somebody's resume.

I read a little bit of it while it was copying.

The person's career objective was "a public relations position allowing for skill enhancement and career growth."

Today as I was getting out of the shower, Mr. Peterson was looking inside the shower cautiously.

When I stepped out, I must have startled her because she ran away really fast.

At the copy store today I had to put finished copies into boxes.

The steady hum of all the copy machines makes the copy store sound like a factory sometimes.

Today Steve told me about a strange experience he had the other day.

He said he was in line at a fast food place when a guy started asking him to fight.

Steve said he was minding his own business, but the guy kept challenging him to a fight.

The guy eventually stopped bugging him, Steve said, but he still felt uncomfortable afterwards.

I made 9,000 copies of an advertising insert today.

When I got home I watched TV, ate a peanut butter and jelly sandwich and got really tired.

Today Tony said he got a job interview with a big company.

"I gotta buy a suit—this is the big time, Jim," he told me.

We went out to get some ice cream.

I got a tutti-frutti cone and Tony said, "How can you get that? That's just about the worst flavor there is!"

Tony had me wish him luck on his big job interview today.

He was wearing his new suit.

I walked around outside for a while.

Then I came back home and watched TV.

I saw Tony today and asked him how it was going.

He said, "Don't ask," and walked into his room.

I saw him later and he told me his job interview yesterday was a disaster.

"The guy didn't even take me seriously," he said.

Today I went out for a walk.

I was cold at first, but got warmer after walking awhile.

I saw a fire hydrant that was painted all different colors.

I also saw a really old man who was hunched over quite a bit.

Today I was making some toast.

When it was finished, it popped out of the toaster hardly toasted at all.

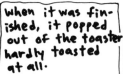

So I put it back in the toaster.

When it popped up again, it was completely burnt.

Today Mr. Peterson woke me up.

I took her into the kitchen and put her by her food.

But she just walked away from it.

I noticed that our kitchen walls are kind of porous.

Today when I fed Mr. Peterson, she just moped and walked away.

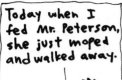

She normally gets really excited when it's time to eat.

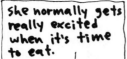

At the copy store today I had to make a whole bunch of copies of something.

They were on 8¼"×14" paper.

Today I noticed that Mr. Peterson has been sitting under my chair all the time.

She hardly ever sits under there.

I picked her up and she seemed really tired.

I felt her paws and her skin was dry and chapped.

I took Mr. Peterson to the veterinarian today.

The waiting room smelled like medicine, and cats and dogs were howling and making noises in the other rooms.

Mr. Peterson was trembling and trying to hide herself in my jacket.

When we went in to see the vet, I told her that Mr. Peterson was acting tired all the time and wasn't eating.

When I came home from the veterinarian yesterday, I ran into Tony.

Tony said, "Hey, how's it goin', cat?"

I told him Mr. Peterson just got some medication from the vet for having a virus.

Tony said his dog back home had heartworm or something and had to eat a huge pill every day.

Today when I fed Mr. Peterson I had to give her some medicine.

She eats it from an eye dropper. It's pink and smells like the veterinarian's office.

She doesn't like it and clenches up her face when I make her swallow it.

The vet said she should eat it for three weeks.

I went to the grocery store with Tony today and he showed me a test for buying frozen pizzas.

"Drop it from five feet up," he said. "If it bounces a little, it's a good one."

Then he said, "There's another test: can you throw it like a frisbee?"

He laughed, and when he saw that I wasn't laughing, he said, "You gotta get a sense of humor, Jim, I swear."

Today I was sitting around not doing much of anything.

Mr. Peterson was playing around, chasing and chewing a kleenex.

I took it away from her because I figured it was bad for her to be eating kleenex.

She did the same running around and playing, only without the kleenex.

Today Ruth and I went out for a walk.

She was telling me a story about something her mom did recently.

She was laughing out loud telling it.

But I didn't think it was all that funny.

Today I decided to clean the kitchen counter under my toaster.

I lifted the toaster up and there was a whole bunch of crumbs.

I dumped the crumbs out of the toaster. There were a lot of them.

Each time I thought I had dumped out all the crumbs, a few more would come out.

This morning Tony pounded on my door and said he forgot to buy food and needed something for breakfast.

"Come on, just anything, Jim," he said.

He looked like he was in a real hurry to get going.

I gave him a box of cereal I had and he said, "Aw, not _this_ stuff!"

Today I was lying on the floor, relaxing.

I was looking at the ceiling, imagining what life would be like if the world was always upside-down.

Mr. Peterson came up to me and sniffed my face.

I could feel her tiny breaths, and her whiskers tickled my face.

Today I was looking up some place in the phone book that I had to call.

While I was flipping through the yellow pages I got sidetracked and just started looking at stuff.

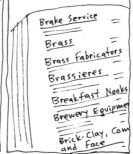

Brake Service

Brass

Brass Fabricators

Brassieres

Breakfast Nooks

Brewery Equipme

Brick-Clay, Com and Face

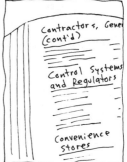

Contractors, Gene (cont'd)

Control Systems and Regulators

Convenience Stores

A comic strip that isn't funny?

With *Jim's Journal* I was trying to parody other comic strips and the comic-strip art form itself. I tried to create a metacomic, one that pointed out the absurdity of the fact that newspapers allot space every day to cartoonists who have nothing to say.

Producing *Jim's Journal* was kind of my way of saying that I don't really like comic strips all that much.

When I set out to parody the form, I thought a good way to start would be to deconstruct standard observational or character-based gags, which were the part of comics I disliked the most—I never thought they were funny. So I set out to communicate the same gags, but in the most unfunny way possible. If such gags were conveyed in very plain language, as a mere existential accounting of the facts, employing no comic timing, poor drawing, and uninteresting subject matter, I thought that would be kind of unexpected and funny. Better still if the strip appeared to say something subtle and true about life, because then it would actually subvert its nominal purpose and transcend the medium.

Creating humor by making fun of other humor is what I call "anti-humor." Not a lot of people appreciate or understand anti-humor. In fact, a lot of people will get really angry when you try it on them. They just want to laugh, they don't want to be part of a humor experiment.

Normally, when people don't like a comic strip, they just ignore it and read other ones. But *Jim's Journal* inspired actual anger. Furious readers wrote letters to the editor. One group of students on the campus of Kansas State University actually began selling "Kill Jim" T-shirts.

That's the power of anti-humor.

Readers who didn't get *Jim's Journal* thought it was an absolute waste of space—even worse than, say, a comic that was trying to be funny and failing. In their minds, *Jim's Journal* wasn't even trying. They thought, Where's the punch line? Why is the drawing so crude? Why is the newspaper even running this!? When, in fact, that illogic was the very thing that was supposed to be funny.

But I know *everybody* has a different sensibility, so it never bothered me that some people hated *Jim's Journal* so passionately. To me, it just meant they didn't appreciate anti-humor.

I like anti-humor, when it's done well. I think it's a much more powerful conduit for a message than regular humor. Some examples of anti-humor I like are Andy Kaufman's stand-up act in which he got up on stage, didn't tell any jokes, and just read *The Great Gatsby*, and Marcel Duchamp's "In Advance of the Broken Arm" (1915), which is a famous work of art displayed in highfalutin art museums, but is just an old snow shovel. (I guess that's more like anti-art, but it's the same principle.)

I worked at the copy store today.

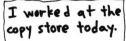

Hal put me to work with someone reorganizing boxes of paper.

We started stacking boxes and she said, "You're new here."

I told her that I suppose you could say I'm new even though I've worked there almost a month.

Today Ruth needed to make some brownies for a friend's birthday party.

I helped her make them.

(I mixed together the brownie mix with the eggs and water and stuff.)

Ruth told me all about her friend— she said she's known her since the third grade.

At the copy store today I was just cleaning up stuff around the floor.

I had to empty the trash, too.

It was really sunny outside, and with all the windows in the copy store, it was really bright in there.

I looked at Hal, who was helping a customer. The sun was shining onto the back of his head and his ear looked bright orange.

Today at the copy store one of the people I work with, Joel, said he was going to San Francisco.

I told him my mom just went to San Francisco for a piano-teachers convention.

He didn't seem too interested.

After I said it I realized it wasn't a very interesting thing to say.

Ruth wanted to go bowling with me and Steve, so we went last night.

It was a lot of fun, even though we weren't any good.

The funniest thing that happened was when Steve let go of his ball wrong.

It rolled straight into the gutter without even touching the lane.

This morning Tony asked me to come over and listen to what happened to him last night.

It was complicated, but centered around his almost getting arrested in front of a bar.

"I met this awesome girl, too—damn, I wish I'd got her name!" he said.

His voice was low and gravelly because of it being so early in the morning.

Today Tony was playing his new tape when it started to slow down.

It slowed down more, then suddenly stopped.

He took it out of the tape player and it was completely unraveled and crumpled.

"Oh, dammit!" he said. "Dammit, dammit, dammit!"

Today Tony was playing another tape and it suddenly slowed to a stop.

"I've had it," he said. "Do you know how many tapes I've lost to this thing?"

He grabbed the machine and smashed it against the wall, the table, and the floor.

Little knobs and stuff shot across the room and the machine got pretty badly bent up.

Julie is one of the people I work with at the copy store.

Today she set the controls for some copies I had to make, and she did it a lot faster than I can.

Hal, the manager, came up to us and said, "As soon as you two are finished here, I've got another job for you."

We both guessed that the job was to make copies on another machine.

I worked at the copy store today.

I had to get up really early to work the morning shift.

I was tired, and just stared into space. I didn't pay attention to what I was doing.

If I relaxed enough, and blocked out all my senses, I could almost sleep standing up.

I was talking with Ruth on the phone today.

She had another call come in and I held on while she found out who it was.

She clicked back to me and said, "I'm back."

(She said the other call was someone for her roommate, who wasn't home.)

I walked into my apartment today and Mr. Peterson came running towards me.

I held out my hands and said, "Hi, Mr. Peterson, come here."

She ran right under me and into the hall.

I tried to coax her back inside, but she liked being out in the hall a lot better.

"Everybody in the whole world has a CD-player except me," Tony said today.

He listed some of the people he knew who had CD-players.

He said he wanted to buy one this friday, at a place that's having a sale.

"What the hell is this cat's problem?" he said.

I went with Tony today to a place where he was going to buy a CD-player.

As we were walking into the store, he said, "The salespeople in these places can be real animals."

He said they practically assault you and sell you things you don't want.

We stood near the CD-players and waited for a salesperson, but nobody came for a long time.

Today I started work at the copy store at 6pm.

As I got there, Hal, Joel and Julie were just leaving.

They looked like they were glad to be done working and going out to have fun.

Brian and I were the only ones working.

(Brian likes to play the radio when he works.)

Today I saw Tony coming home.

He was carrying a little plastic bag.

He didn't say anything as he walked past me. He just jiggled the bag and smiled.

I could see that it had a CD in it.

Today I worked the evening shift with Brian at the copy store.

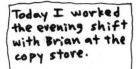

Hardly anybody came in.

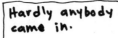

Brian and I didn't have much work to do.

He asked me if I'd mind if he turned the radio up louder and I said not really.

It was really cold today so I wore a hat.

When I took it off I could feel that part of my hair was sticking up.

At night I was just lying in bed.

I touched my head and found that my hair was still sticking up in that spot.

Today I was throwing around a little ball for Mr. Peterson.

I was trying to throw it right to her so she'd catch it.

But she would bat it away instead.

Also today I watched "The Flash" on TV and even though Steve doesn't like the show, I thought it was okay.

Today I was walking outside for a while.

It was snowing.

I saw some people playing and throwing snowballs at each other.

(I was on the other side of the street, so I didn't get hit with any snowballs.)

I went to the store today to buy some food.

Isle 6

While I was waiting in line I looked at the tabloids.

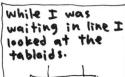

Express Lane
12 Items or less

There was a story about a werewolf baby that was pretty funny.

Express Lane
12 Items or less

After a while a woman standing in front of me said, "This express lane isn't very expressive, is it?"

12 Items or less

I ate lunch with Ruth today.

She was telling me what her ten favorite popular songs were.

(she was trying to list them in order, one through ten.)

When she finished, she thought maybe she should switch songs nine and ten around.

I walked by somebody on the sidewalk today.

He was a big guy who stood there and smiled as I walked past him.

"It's a miracle," he said, "Life is a miracle!"

I didn't respond to him and kept walking, but I kept hearing him in my head over and over.

I got up early for work today.

I fed Mr. Peterson. She was really hungry, as always.

At the copy store I made 200 copies of some kind of office report.

I pictured Mr. Peterson eating, bobbing her head like she does.

At the copy store today a customer wanted me to make a copy for her.

So I did.

She handed me a dollar bill that had a ripped corner.

She asked if we could accept it and I said I guess we could.

Mr. Peterson ran out the door again when I came home today.

I let her stay in the hall for a while, and she seemed very interested in exploring.

Then, down the hall, somebody closed a door and the noise startled her.

She ran inside and stayed there

Today I was walking outside.

While I was walking I saw someone walking toward me.

Suddenly he turned around and started walking in the opposite direction.

I guess he must have forgotten something.

Today at the copy store Hal, the manager, was working along with everybody else.

He likes to laugh and kid around a lot.

But whenever he does, he ends it by saying, "Alright, enough monkeying around, let's get back to work."

He doesn't say it in those exact words every time, but generally that's what he does.

I sat in bed this morning before I got up and pictured myself as infinitely big one second, then as small as a pea the next. This happened over and over, like a strobe light, for about 20 seconds.

I visited Ruth today.

When I came to her apartment she apologized for it being such a mess.

But it looked perfectly clean and tidy to me.

I worked at the copy store today.

I overheard Hal talking to someone about Brian being "on thin ice."

I guessed that Hal thought Brian was doing a bad job, even though I'd never noticed.

I worked with Brian that night and kept thinking about what Hal said.

Today I decided to vacuum my floor. 	Mr. Peterson hid under the table and watched the vacuum cleaner intently. 	When I headed toward her, she got scared and ran away. 	
I worked at the copy store with Brian last night. 	I noticed he was making some two-sided copies with one side upside-down. 	I pointed it out to him and he said, "Oops," then chuckled. 	I wondered if I would have noticed his mistake if I hadn't heard Hal talking about Brian doing a bad job.
Mr. Peterson was taking a nap on the floor today. 	She was sleeping in a spot where the sun was shining through the window. 	She stretched herself out and then turned up on her back. 	Then suddenly she looked at me and said, "Pleep!" 
Today Steve came over and said he was getting rid of all his Spider Man comic books. 	He asked if I wanted them and I said no. 	I asked him why he was getting rid of them. 	And he said he just couldn't think of any reason to have them. 

Today I was walking home from work at night.	I looked up at the sky while I walked.	I realized it'd been a long time since I just looked at the sky.	I thought maybe I've been cooped up too much lately.

I had to get up early today to go work at the copy store.	I really didn't feel like getting up at all.	But I did anyway because I had to.	After I was up for a while I wasn't that tired anymore.

Today at the copy store Julie was making copies.	She was stacking up all the finished copies, too.	Then she exhaled a really long, slow breath.	I could hear it over the hum of all the machines even where I was standing.

I ran into the guy from down the hall today.	I was walking in and passed him by the door.	"How's the weather out there today?" he said.	I told him it was okay.

Today Tony, Steve and I went to a movie.

Tony got some milk duds and a Pepsi and said, "Nature's perfect food!"

Steve went to the rest rooms and Tony said, "What's he doing? The movie's gunna start any second."

Steve came back right when the movie started.

Today I went to visit Ruth.

On top of her TV I noticed some clay casts of teeth.

She's a dental assistant, so I thought they were things she got from her job.

But she said they were casts of her own teeth, "when I was 5, 12 and 17 years old," she said.

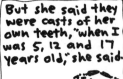

I worked at the copy store almost eight hours today.

When I got home I was really tired.

I moved the TV next to my bed so I could lie down, relax, and watch whatever was on.

This morning before I woke up I had a strange dream.

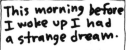

I was in a big building full of people that was having a really loud fire alarm.

The alarm sounded a lot like Mr. Peterson meowing.

Then I realized it was just a dream and that Mr. Peterson was probably meowing right next to my ear.

Today Ruth and I went over to see Steve.

He was eating an apple when we came in.

"To what do I owe the pleasure of your company?" he asked.

We said we just stopped by—no particular reason.

Today Brian said his friend was in a band and was performing at a bar that night.

He said, "It should be a good show—I'm excited about it."

I was making some copies that came out with little black splotches on them.

I wiped off the glass and that took care of the problem.

I was sitting around today feeling pretty bored.

Mr. Peterson walked by me a couple times, meowing to herself.

Then she hopped up on the chair and sat in my lap, but didn't sleep.

I guess she was feeling bored today too.

Today at the copy store things were really slow.

Brian asked me if I'd mind if he smoked, and I said not really.

Then someone came in to make some self-service copies and asked Brian if he'd mind putting out his cigarette.

Brian said, "Hey, sure, man. No problem. That's cool," and put it out.

At the copy store today Brian and I were preparing a bunch of copies for somebody.

Brian suddenly said, "I don't feel like doing this," and went over by the counter.

I asked him why he doesn't seem to like working here very much.

He said, "It's not my copy store—I can only care so much."

I came home today around 6 p.m.

When I opened the door, Mr. Peterson shot outside really fast.

I went to get her and she cowered away from me like she was afraid for her life.

Once I got her back inside, she sat by the door and meowed.

Ruth came over to visit today.

She picked up Mr. Peterson and said, "Hello there!"

Mr. Peterson stared at Ruth with a surprised, wide-eyed look on her face.

Ruth stared back at Mr. Peterson with the same wide-eyed look.

Today I walked by the bookstore where I used to work.

I started remembering all the times I spent there.

I didn't really like working there back then, but for some reason I had nice memories of it.

I sat around and watched TV today.

After a while I got bored with the TV so I turned it off.

While I sat there, I started to feel like I was floating.

I sat around and watched TV for a while today.

I watched Unsolved Mysteries and they had a story about a UFO landing in Pennsylvania.

They made it sound like it could have actually happened.

I thought it was a pretty good show.

Today Tony came by and said, "Hey, Jim, you're gonna love this..."

He had a little rubber puppet thing that was just a face that contorted when he moved his fingers.

Tony growled when the face looked angry, hollered when the face's mouth was wide open, and had fun making silly faces with it.

"Isn't this just the greatest thing?" he said.

When I came home today I noticed the light by my door was burned out.

I had a hard time trying to find my key because it was so dark.

I thought I should call the landlord about it.

But I didn't feel like doing it right then.

When I came home today I had to try to find my keys in the dark hallway.

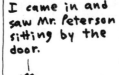

I came in and saw Mr. Peterson sitting by the door.

I sat there and petted her for a while.

Today Tony told me about a dream he had last night.

"It was wild, Jim, you wouldn't have believed it," he said.

He said he had a race car that could take him anywhere in the world in 2 seconds.

"But the weird thing is," he said, "I only went to my Aunt Helen's house and a meat-packing plant."

I worked at the copy store today and a lot of people were coming in.

I made tons of copies and worked the cash register, too.

Once I noticed Ruth walking by outside.

She didn't see me, and I was too busy to stop and talk or anything anyway.

As I was coming home today I saw the guy from down the hall.

He was walking more slowly than usual.

He walked by me without saying anything.

I tried to find my door key in the dark hall.

(I still haven't called the landlord about the burned-out light.)

I worked at the copy store today.

I was there earlier than I usually am.

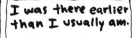

Hal, the manager, Julie, and Joel were all there.

Things weren't as laid back as when just Brian and I are working the evening shift.

Today Tony was walking home with me.

We got to my door and I couldn't find my key right away because the hall light is burned out.

"You should call the landlord about that," Tony said.

When we got inside, Tony told me he has a good chance of working at an ad agency.

Today I was just sitting around.

Then Tony came by.

He said he looked into the ad agency job he was hoping to get.

"All they want is some stooge to sit in the xerox room all day and make copies!" he said.

Tony was talking today about the ad agency job he was trying to get.

He said he couldn't believe the job was in the xerox room and not in the sales or creative dept.

"I have a college education for Pete's sake!" he said. "In economics!"

"I know all about money and ads and stuff."

Today I got up a little late. 	The clock-radio alarm went off about a half hour before I got up. 	Somehow I slept through it and didn't even hear it. 	I fed Mr. Peterson and she ate up her food like crazy. 
Today I was bored and was just sitting up on my big chair.	I started to rock the chair back and forth. 	I felt like I was going to fall over any minute. 	when I eventually did, it didn't hurt or anything. It was even kind of fun.
I worked at the copy store today. 	But I didn't really feel like I was there. 	My body did all the walking around and making copies. 	But my mind was somewhere else. 
I went to the pet store today to get more food for Mr. Peterson. 	They had some new kittens there, so I looked at them for a while. 	They were asleep, and didn't move much when I touched them. 	I couldn't believe how small they were. 

I got up and sat around this morning.

Then I went to the copy store and worked from noon to 5:30.

Then I came home and watched TV for a while.

When the day was over, it struck me how unremarkable a day it had been.

This morning I was lying in bed trying to sleep.

But Mr. Peterson was walking around meowing.

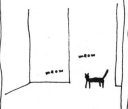

Once, she hopped up right in front of me and looked at me.

I asked her what the heck she was meowing about and she just meowed again.

As I was coming home today I noticed a repairman in the hall.

He was replacing the light bulb by my door.

I kept forgetting to call the landlord about it.

I guess they found out about it from somebody else.

Today I went to Tony's apartment and he was watching TV.

He was flipping between the channels with his remote control.

He was flipping through channels faster and faster.

Finally he just held down the channel-changing button—the channels flipped by so fast the screen was just a blur.

Today I was making copies of a story somebody wrote.

I thought it might be fun to read while I copied it.

But I was copying it too fast, so I couldn't have kept up with it even if I'd wanted to.

So I just stood there and stared off into space.

Today at the copy store one of the copy machines broke down.

Hal took a look at it and said he knew what the problem was.

He stuck a pen in there and poked it around.

Everybody stood around and watched him even though it wasn't very interesting.

Steve came by today.

"How's it goin', Mr. P," he said to Mr. Peterson.

She completely ignored him and walked right by.

"Hey, Jim, guess what I did," he said, and then he told me he signed up for a sailboating class.

I saw the guy from down the hall today.

He passed by me and said, "How are you today," in a really loud voice.

I said I was fine.

"Hard not to be on a day like today, eh?"

(It was a nice and sunny day today.)

Today I walked by a fast food restaurant.

It had a big sign in the window that said "Now Hiring."

But the window frame blocked part of the sign so it looked like "Now Firing."

I thought that was kind of funny.

Today I started thinking about what it would be like if I worked at the copy store my whole life.

I'd be the manager and I'd know everything about the store.

I don't know why I was thinking about it.

It was kind of depressing.

Today when I came to work Brian wasn't there.

I asked where he was and somebody said, "He quit."

"He's lucky he quit when he did," Hal said, "'cause he was on his last leg anyway."

It struck me what a tough, cutthroat place the copy store really is.

Today at the copy store Julie and I were the only ones working.

I was on the cash register and Julie was making copies.

I asked if she'd mind switching jobs for a while and she said, "oh, great."

I couldn't tell if she was being serious or completely sarcastic.

I was outside walking around today.

I noticed a delivery truck or something parked on the street.

I looked up close at one of the tires.

It had a lot of ridges, and little things that looked like tiny rubber whiskers sticking out of it.

I hung around with Ruth today.

We took a bus to a mall.

(She likes to go to malls to look at stuff.)

When we were in the mall she said, "I bet they have a store for everything here."

Today I worked at the copy store all day.

I came home and was so tired I just fell right onto my bed and fell asleep.

I woke up at 2 a.m. and was wide awake.

There was nothing else to do, so I played with Mr. Peterson till dawn.

When I woke up today I was lying on the floor with Mr. Peterson snuggled into my neck.

I looked at the clock and saw that it was noon.

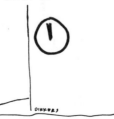

I was supposed to be at work at 9 a.m., so I hurried to the copy store.

When I got there Hal said, "Jim—we all thought you were dead."

I was glad that he didn't seem to care that I was so late.

This morning at the copy store a lot of people were working.

I was kind of tired, and we were disorganized and bumping into each other.

Hal came up from the back room and clapped his hands and said. "Let's go, gang— look alive!"

I suddenly felt even more tired than I did before.

Today I sat on a bench and ate an apple.

It was a nice sunny day and a lot of people were outside.

Someone with a little girl walked by me and the girl was looking at me.

Then she smiled and tried to hide behind her mom so I couldn't see her.

Today I was getting something to drink from a pop machine with Tony.

I put my money in and the can came right out.

Tony put his coins in, pushed the knob, and nothing happened. "Oh, no!" he said.

Then, after a couple seconds, the can came tumbling down. "Whew!" Tony said.

I decided to go out and visit my mom for a while.

"Nice of you to drop by once every eon or so," she said.

She asked how everything was going and I said everything was going fine.

Her cookie jar was full of cream-filled oatmeal cookies.

Today my mom showed me a bunch of pictures from her trip to San Francisco.

She told me how much fun she had and how nice the city was.

She had a new story to tell for each picture.

After that I took a nap.

Last night I slept in my mom's guest room.

It's kept clean and perfectly neat when no one's in it.

I felt like I was trashing it just by being there.

When I got up today my mom was out doing something.

(She left a note.)

I went over to my dad's house today.

"Well, hello there," my dad said.

He took me behind his house to show me a new thing he just bought that he said he was really excited about.

It was a big motorcycle.

I came back home today after visiting my parents.

Ruth was in my apartment.

(She took care of Mr. Peterson while I was gone.)

She hugged Mr. Peterson and said, "She's been such a good kitty."

Then Mr. Peterson jumped out of her arms and ran away and hid.

I Made Some Brownies

My third *Jim's Journal* collection was called *I Made Some Brownies and they were pretty good*. As the book was taking shape, I figured I had already put Jim through college, I had already given him a job. What else was there? Anything more, like marriage, having kids, or any other big life change, seemed inconceivable for low-key Jim. So, I figured he should just enjoy some brownies.

And this is a subject close to my heart. One of my favorite things to do is make a pan of brownies and spend a few days holed up at home, sitting around, watching TV, and eating nothing but brownies.

I got up pretty early this morning.

while I opened Mr. Peterson's food, she walked back and forth, rubbing up against my legs, meowing.

Sometimes she wouldn't so much rub as slam the side of her body into my leg.

I worked at the copy store from 9 to noon.

Today I went to visit Ruth.

We walked around by where she lives.

We saw some kids playing in a playground.

And a big truck.

Today when I came home my clock was flashing 12:00.

I figured there was probably a power outage or something

So I reset it.

A guy came into the copy store today and told me he forgot his original in our copy machine.

I looked in the lost-n-found box and couldn't find it.

I told him that people lose their originals there all the time.

But his was important, he said.

Steve called me today just to see what I was doing.	I said I wasn't doing much of anything. 	"Well, maybe we could get together and do something," he said. 	We came up with a lot of ideas for what we could do, but neither of us felt like doing any of them.
Today Steve came over and said, "Happy birthday, Jim," and handed me a present.	I told him my birthday was yesterday and he said, "Yeah, well, here's a present anyway." 	 crackle crumple rip	It was an address book. 
Today I decided to write down some addresses of people in my new address book. 	I wrote down my mom's, dad's, grandma's... 	Then Tony's, Ruth's, Steve's... 	I suddenly realized that I hardly know anybody at all. 
Today Steve, Ruth and I were sitting around talking about bugs, among other things. 	Ruth said, "There's nothing worse than having a mosquito buzzing around your ear." 	"Except having your knee caps sawed off maybe," Steve said. 	"That's awful," Ruth said. "How could you even think of such a thing?" 

Today Tony came by and said he played pool the other day. "It was great," he said.

He asked me if I wanted to play pool with him.

I said sure, why not.

While we played, Tony licked his lip and concentrated really hard when he shot.

I played pool with Tony again today.

Whenever he would make a shot, he'd say, "Alright! That was somethin', eh, Jim?"

But when he'd miss several shots in a row, he'd say, "Geez, what's wrong with me? This is ridiculous!"

While we were walking out of the pool hall, he said, "Pool is just the coolest sport, isn't it?"

I said I thought it was okay.

Today I was pouring myself a glass of water.

Mr. Peterson was standing behind me, looking at me.

She looked like she was just curious about what I was doing, so I showed her the water.

Today I noticed my clock was flashing 12:00 again.

I checked to see if it was fully plugged in.

It was.

I couldn't figure out what was the matter with it.

Ruth moved out of her apartment today, and I helped her.

She had all her stuff packed into boxes and ready to go.

She kept mentioning her sofa and how she was worried about how we would get it to fit through the door.

But when the time came to take it away, it was no problem at all.

I went over to help Ruth again today.

She was in her new place but wanted help unpacking things.

She had all the boxes sorted in each respective room.

But before we did any work, she made lemonade and we sat and relaxed.

I was just lying in bed today when I started getting really sleepy.

I half-fell asleep, thinking about boxes being packed, and having little dreams where I had to make sure everything was packed right.

I woke up when a car horn honked continuously for about two minutes, right outside my window.

Honk

I got out of bed and was so dazed I could barely walk without falling.

Today I was eating a cheese sandwich when I noticed my clock was completely blank.

Then, after a minute, it started to flash 12:00 for a while, then it went off again.

I went over to see what was going on.

I saw Mr. Peterson wrestling with the cord, making it move slightly in and out of the socket.

Tony came by today.

I thought he'd want to play pool, but he said, "Ah, I'm sick of pool."

We ended up watching the news on TV.

Tony pointed at the newscaster and said, "Get a loada that guy's hair!"

Today I bought a rotating thing for the microwave that runs on batteries.

I heated up some beans and watched them turn around slowly on the rotating thing.

They started bubbling after a few seconds.

After they were done and the oven turned off, I kept watching them turn around for a while.

I came home from the copy store today, made a peanut butter sandwich, and watched TV.

When I was done eating I felt really tired.

After a while, I realized I wasn't paying attention to the TV, but I didn't have enough energy to turn it off.

At the copy store today we got a shipment of paper.

I helped unload it from the truck.

Julie was standing by the back door, where we were stacking the boxes.

"oh good," she said, "more paper."

I went walking around today.

I walked by a big corporate headquarters of a bank or something.

They had patches of grass and some potted trees in a big cement area by the main entrance.

I sat there for a while and watched people with suits and hard shoes walk briskly in and out.

Today Tony drove me around because he had his brother's car for the day.

"We'll go cruisin' for chicks!" he said.

We stopped at a red light and Tony tapped his hands on the wheel.

We sat there a long time and Tony yelled, "come on—change!" and then the light finally changed.

I was trying to open my window today to get a little breeze.

But it wouldn't stay open by itself.

So I put a book under it to hold it open.

Then Mr. Peterson and I sat there and just looked out the window for a while.

I went to a gift shop with Ruth today.

She bought a calendar with pictures of puppies and kittens on it.

"They're so cute," she said. "I just love 'em!"

She told me she almost got the "Rear View" calendar.

Tony came by today to tell me he had a girl-friend.

"I really think this is it, Jim. I think I'm in love," he said.

I asked him what her name was and he said, "Jaime—I mean Jill. It's Jill."

He realized how funny it was to stumble on the word. "Yeah, duh—I can't even say her name," he said

Tony brought his new girlfriend, Jill, over today.

"Jill, I just wanted you to meet my buddy, Jim," he said.

We said hi to each other.

After a few seconds, Tony said, "I just wanted you two to meet."

Today Ruth and I ate at a pan-cake restaurant.

While we were waiting for our food, we read the paper placemats.

On the backs they had games and puzzles for kids to play.

Ruth wanted to play the dot-to-dot but neither of us had a pen.

I let Mr. Peterson outside for a little while today.

Like usual, she was really scared, and stayed pretty much in one place.

But she eventually explored all the stairs near the door.

After she did that, she went back to her space and stayed there.

Today I went out on a bike ride. 	I stopped by a ball park and watched part of a little league game or something. 	I liked the way the sound of the bat hitting the ball echoed across the park. 	It was almost dark by the time I got back home. 
I saw Tony today on the way to my mailbox. 	He was with his new girlfriend, Jill. 	They both said "Hi, Jim," in unison as they passed me. 	I got my mail and all I got was a flyer about a missing child. 
I got a newspaper today and sat at the table to read it. 	Mr. Peterson jumped up on the table and stood on the newspaper. 	I put her back on the floor. 	Then she ran into the other room and meowed over and over. 
Today Ruth and I went driving around. 	She was running a bunch of errands and I just came along. 	We went to a couple of stores, the post office, and places like that. 	When we were done, Ruth said, "That was kind of fun, wasn't it?" 

I decided to start reading a book today.	It's I, Robot, by Isaac Asimov. (Steve told me it was a pretty good book and I should read it.)	when I sat down to read, Mr. Peterson was sitting on the table, just across the room from me. 	Every time I would try to start reading, Mr. Peterson would look at the ceiling and meow, and I couldn't concentrate. 
I read some more of my book today. 	(It's I, Robot.)		So far, I think it's a pretty good book.
Today I had to clean my kitchen. 	I scrubbed out the sink, mopped the floor, and everything. 	Mr. Peterson watched, but was too scared to get any closer than a couple of yards away. 	After I was done, she cautiously stepped into the kitchen, sniffing the floor and the air.
I was woken up today by the phone ringing. 	It was somebody I didn't recognize saying, "Al—you slept in, huh, ace?" 	After that, I tried to get back to sleep, but couldn't. 	Mr. Peterson was scratching the wall, something was tapping on the ceiling—every little noise seemed extra loud. 

I finished reading I, Robot today.

It was a short book, so it didn't take me very long to read it.

Steve, who was the one who told me I should read it, said, "How'd you like it?"

I said I thought it was a pretty good book.

Today I felt like eating a fried egg.

It'd been so long since I had a fried egg that for a second I couldn't think of how to make one.

But it was only for a second.

Once I realized I knew how to do it, I knew it was really easy.

I saw Tony and Jill again today.

They both said hi to me as I passed them.

Later in the day Tony stopped by.

"Jim," he said, "you ever know somebody who did little things that just bugged you?"

I saw Tony today. He had just come back from picking up his mail.

I asked him where Jill was.

"You don't wanna know," he said.

He flipped through his mail to see what he got.

At the copy store today I worked with Hal.

While he was looking at the copy we made, I noticed how tightly curled his hair is.

He showed me some paste-up marks he found on the copy, and told me to touch them up.

"This wouldn't happen if we had one of those Canon 6650's," he said."

I was walking outside today when I noticed a squirrel by a tree.

He looked at me, then ran up the tree.

Then I came home and saw Mr. Peterson.

She dashed out the door as soon as I opened it.

I walked past my chair today and noticed Mr. Peterson chewing on it.

When she saw me she ran away.

I sat down to watch some TV.

Nothing was on.

Today Tony told me he had decided to get a better job.

(For the past few months he's been working at the shoe store where his brother's the manager.)

"There's no future in shoes," he said.

He asked if I'd help him write a resumé and I said I would.

I made myself a peanut butter and jelly sandwich today and sat down to eat it.

I thought I'd listen to the radio while I ate.

I tuned in a few stations to find something good.

But nothing good was on.

I helped Tony with his resumé today.

We sat around and tried to make his job experiences sound really good.

He was getting frustrated because he's only worked at a grocery store, an ice rink and the shoe store.

"These jobs make me sound like just some boob who's never accomplished anything!" he said.

I helped Tony work on his resumé again today.

Tony said we should work on sharpening up the fine points.

(He was eating a Hostess pie.)

"Like this," he said. "Instead of 'worked' at ice rink, say 'organized' or 'managed.'"

He also said that when he takes it to the printer, he'll pick out a type style that will fix up the whole thing.

I got up early today and was really tired.

I fed Mr. Peterson, took a shower, and ate some cereal...

But even then I was still really tired.

So I slept for a little while longer.

I was walking home from work today when I realized I forgot my coat.

It was a pretty nice day outside, and I didn't really need a coat.

But I went back to the copy store to pick it up anyway.

Julie was there, and didn't even notice that I'd come back.

There was somebody new at the copy store today.

Hal said, "Dan just started today— will you show him how to work the big copier?"

I showed him what all the buttons and dials did, and how to set them.

I explained how to enlarge, reduce, collate, change trays, and everything.

Dan was working at the copy store again today.

He was having trouble making a copy, so I showed him how to do it again.

"Oh, yeah, of course. I forgot that part," he said.

I felt really tired that night, and fell asleep really early.

Today I was tired, so I fell down onto my bed.

I thought I might fall asleep.

But Mr. Peterson walked onto my back and started kneading me with her paws.

Her claws were sharp and there was no way I could fall asleep with her doing that.

Today I made a peanut butter and jelly sandwich and sat down to eat it.

I put a lot of jelly on it and it started oozing onto the plate.

I turned the sandwich over so the big clumps of jelly would be on top.

But then it started to ooze out the bottom.

I slept in late today and felt really tired.

I probably got too much sleep.

I had my lunch break with Dan today.

He told me there were seven kids in his family, and he was number five.

I slept in late again today.

I just really felt like sleeping.

Normally that feeling wears off during the day.

But today I felt tired all day.

I got out my big winter coat today.

After I put it on I found a dollar bill in the pocket.

I didn't remember putting it there last winter, so it was kind of a nice little surprise.

I ran into Tony and he said, "The world might as well end right now, Jim."

Today I was talking to Tony.

He was telling me all about the hard time he was having finding a job.

"I sent all my resumés out, but nobody's calling!" he said.

He told me he doesn't think he can stand his brother's shoe store for one more day.

Today at the copy store, Joel was showing Dan how to fill the copier with toner.

He explained it kind of quickly and then told Dan to try it.

Dan didn't do it right and Joel said, "c'mon, it's simple," and explained it again.

"I can't teach this guy anything," he said.

Today I noticed Mr. Peterson batting something around on the floor, so I picked it up.

She backed up and got ready to pounce, as if waiting for me to throw it back to her.

I looked closely at it and it was a thin blue plastic thing with a little ridge on the end.

I couldn't imagine where it came from.

Today I decided to visit Tony at the shoe store where he works.

It's in a mall, and nobody was in the store when I came.

"That's the best thing about working here," Tony said, "no customers."

He also said, "I gotta get outta here, man. This place is killin' me."

I was making copies with Julie today.

We put the finished copies into crates, and Julie carried them into the back, by the loading dock.

Every time she lifted one or put one down, she grunted and groaned.

She asked how many boxes we had left to fill and I said eight, and she made a really long steady groan.

I washed some clothes today.

While I was in the laundry room I noticed a shirt on the floor.

It looked like it was a perfectly good shirt.

But it was full of dirt and lint and was discarded in a corner behind a trash can.

I saw Tony today. He said somebody called him for a job interview.

"I sent out fifty resumes last month," he said, "It's about time somebody called."

He said the call was from a shoe store on the other end of town.

"This is great!" he said. "Working there would be a million times better than working at my brother's shoe store."

Tony had his interview at the other shoe store today.

I asked him how it went and he said, "It went fine."

But by the way he said it, it didn't sound like it went fine.

Today I saw a guy picking coins out of the snow by a parking meter.

"I need to rethink my whole life—everything," Tony said today.

He said he realized that moving from one shoe store to another wasn't the way to get ahead.

He said, "It took me a long time to realize this."

I asked him what his big plans were and he said he didn't know.

Today Ruth came over and showed me the new coat she got.

It had a special kind of soft lining on the inside.

She said it was on sale and she couldn't pass it up.

She hung it on a chair and Mr. Peterson tried to climb up inside it.

I just sat around today and didn't do much of anything.

It was kind of rainy outside.

I thought of taking a nap, but I wasn't very tired.

So I just sat around and didn't do much of anything.

I was walking home today when I noticed somebody waiting at a bus stop.

She said, "Say, do you know when the B bus is supposed to get here?"

I told her I didn't know.

"It's late," she said. "It should've been here by now—I'm sure of it."

I didn't have to work at the copy store today so I slept in.

I woke up a few times, but never felt like getting out of bed.

After a while I realized I was sleeping even when I didn't feel like sleeping any more.

When I finally got up, it was 1:30.

Today I saw a guy in an old army coat walk into an ice cream store.

He was unshaven and looked like he was shaking out of nervousness or something.

I thought for a moment about the possibility that he would go in the store and shoot everybody.

But I figured the chance of that happening was pretty slim.

I was just sitting around today when mr. Peterson came up and sat on my lap.

I scratched her back and she purred.

She looked at me and closed her eyes then opened them, like a slow-motion blink.

Then she got comfortable and fell asleep.

Today I saw Tony and he asked how it was going.

I said it was going fine.

He said he'd be quitting his shoe-store job any day now, "then look out, world!" he said.

I went home and ate a bowl of soup.

I went to the bookstore today to find a book to read.

I couldn't find anything that I felt like reading.

While I was walking home I noticed a torn piece of newspaper on the sidewalk.

I stood there for a while and read it.

I got some tacos for lunch today.

Dan came with me.

As we sat down, we noticed that we both ordered two soft tacos and a coke.

Dan commented on how most of the people in line seemed to prefer soft tacos to the hard-shelled kind.

Today at the copy store Hal came up to me and said, "Hey, Jim, how's it goin'?"

I said everything was going fine.

He stood there for a while, kind of looking around.

Then he swept some eraser shavings off the counter top with his hand.

While I was taking a shower today the soap slipped out of my hands and flew onto the floor.

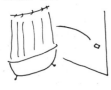

Mr. Peterson heard it fall and came over to smell it.

I looked at her, wondering if maybe she would bat it over to me.

And she ran away from it really fast.

Today at the copy store Hal tuned the radio to a different station than usual.

But nobody else liked the station.

"Come on—this music is just fine," Hal said. "Now get back to work."

They kept bugging him, so he finally changed it back, saying, "Alright, alright, you whiners."

Today Tony told me he was going to be a millionaire in ten years.

"It's all right here in this awesome book," he said.

He showed me the part of the book that explained how to save and get interest so you can make a million dollars.

"This guy's a genius, Jim," he said. "This can't fail."

Today Hal called the newspaper to place a want ad for somebody to work weekdays.

When he hung up he said, "Jim, if you know anybody, tell 'em to apply."

When I got home I sat down with a plate of cookies to watch TV.

There was a show on that was predicting what life would be like in the next century.

I was sitting around today when Mr. Peterson started rubbing against me.

I scratched her head for a while and she purred like crazy.

Suddenly she popped her head up and stopped purring, as if she'd heard something in the other room.

She ran into the other room as fast as she could.

At the copy store today I worked with Julie.

I worked the cash register for all the self-service customers that came in.

Julie was making a bunch of copies of something that were due the next day.

When I heard the machine stop, I looked at Julie and she looked like she was asleep.

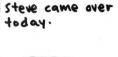

Steve came over today.

Mr. Peterson looked up at him and meowed a big bellowing meow when he came in.

Steve said "Yeah, life is hard, isn't it? I know."

Mr. Peterson meowed again.

Today Tony told me he needed to find another part-time job.

"If I'm gonna use this millionaire strategy, I need to put away a little bit more every month," he said.

I thought of telling him about Hal's copy store job, but figured he wouldn't be interested.

"I'm gonna look into something in radio or TV," he said.

I was talking with Dan a little bit today.

He told me he had once considered a career in the sciences.

"Science is like math," he said, "it's black and white—no gray areas."

And that's why he likes science, he said.

Today I watched TV for a while.

Then I went for a walk.

When I came back home and hung up my coat, the coat hook came out of the wall.

Around the inside edges of the little hole I could see tiny bits of plaster and wood.

Today I got off work at the copy store at 5:30.

While I was walking, a snowball suddenly hit me in the back of the head.

Then I heard somebody laughing, so I turned around to look at her.

"Gotchya!" she said.

Today I went to a craft & hobby shop with Ruth. 	(She had to buy some felt.) 	She picked out the felt she wanted and went up to the cashier.	I waited in line with her and looked at the ceramic lawn gnomes. 
I washed a load of laundry today. 	After taking the clothes out of the dryer, I brought them up to my apartment. 	I was going to put them away, but Mr. Peterson jumped in the basket and got comfortable. 	So I decided to put them away later. 
Today Ruth showed me the thing she made with the felt she bought. 	It was a sign that she made for her friend Janet. 	It said, "A true friend is the greatest gift of all." 	She explained how she glued the felt, some sparklers, and other things all together. 
Today I was just sitting at my table, feeling kind of tired and bored. 	I rested my head on my arms and started to doze. 	Then Mr. Peterson jumped on the table. I could hear her purring. 	Then she walked up onto my back and just sat there. 

Today Steve rented a movie and he invited me over to watch it.	It was Ben Hur.	It was about 3 hours long, and we watched the whole thing.	When it was over, Steve said, "I thought it would be retro-funny, but it was actually good."

Today Tony said "Hey—I'm going to Santa Monica for my brother's friend's wedding... wanna come?"	I said I would.	"Cool," he said. Then he told me all about the places we could go and things we could see.	"Oh—I should tell you," he said, "we leave tomorrow at 8 a.m."

Today Tony, his brother Mike and I got into Mike's car and headed for Santa Monica, CA.	Tony and Mike ate Doritos and talked a lot about the shoe store where they work.	The smell of vinyl seats started to make me feel a little carsick.	Tony turned to me and said, "Plenty of Doritos, Jim—dig in!"

We've been taking turns sleeping and driving in shifts.	Today, for a while, Tony was sleeping in the back seat and I was sitting in front with his brother Mike.	Even though I don't know Mike at all, we managed to have a conversation by talking about Tony.	When we ran out of things to say about Tony, we didn't say anything.

We arrived in Santa Monica last night.

Today Mike went off with his friend, and Tony and I went driving around the city.

Tony said, "Can you believe we're in sunny Californ-I-A? And on shoe store money!"

We tried driving up to the Hollywood sign, but we couldn't find the road up to it.

Today Tony and I went to Disneyland.

We waited in line for a long time for all the rides.

"The problem is, too many damned idiots come to this place!" Tony said.

We liked the Magic Mountain and Star Tours rides the best.

Today was Mike's friend's wedding, and Tony and Mike both went.

I sat around his house, where we were staying, and watched TV.

Then I went to the beach, which is only a few blocks from his house.

I listened to the ocean and watched all the people walking around.

We left Santa Monica today.

Nobody was saying much, and I got the impression Mike hadn't had a good time.

When Tony started to say something about it, Mike interrupted, saying "Shut up, Tony. I don't wanna hear it."

We drove all night and into the next day, in shifts.

When I walked up to my apartment today, Steve was just coming out of it.

(He took care of Mr. Peterson while I was gone.)

"Hey, Jim!" he said. "How was your big trip?"

I said it was pretty good.

I bought a Newsweek magazine today so I'd have something to read.

While I was walking home, I walked behind two people who were talking about their friends.

"I don't really have just, like, one best friend," one of them said.

"But I have, like, a bunch of really close friends, y'know?" she said.

Today I called to get a pizza delivered, with extra sauce, cheese and mushrooms.

The guy who delivered it was wearing a hat with the pizza company's logo on it.

I sat down and ate my pizza and read my Newsweek magazine.

I thought maybe they forgot to put the extra sauce on my pizza, but I couldn't really tell.

I worked at the copy store today.

Afterwards, I walked home the long way, by the lake.

There were people walking around the lake, and ducks sitting on the shore.

I decided to sit and watch people go by, and listen to the ducks.

Jim's Pre-History

Writing and drawing a comic strip, and actually managing to eke out a living at it, had been a lifelong dream of mine since as far back as I can remember.

My best friend in childhood was Marcellus Hall, who has since become a successful illustrator (and lead singer of the band Railroad Jerk). Marce and I, in fourth and third grade respectively, would hang out after school and draw comics and read *Mad* magazine. I was dazzled by Marce's drawing skill. He and I tried to copy the styles of all our favorite artists from *Mad*, such as Jack Davis, Mort Drucker, Don Martin, and Sergio Aragones. But mostly, I copied Marce. Duly inspired, I produced dozens of complete little cartoon books out of small spiral-bound notebooks. Some were cartoon ABC books, others had continuous story lines.

I mostly gave up the idea of cartooning when I moved away from home when I was eighteen. Partly I was rebelling against everyone's expectations (my whole family seemed to think I should be a cartoonist), but mostly I became more interested in making movies. I made some short films and was always plotting something bigger. I even went so far as to transfer to the University of Southern California, in the hope of getting into the film school there. But the realities of having to pay the rent and feed myself began to slowly encroach as I spent less time making money and more time making budget-breaking super-8 movies.

While at USC, I must have had a lot of cartooning tendencies in me, because I doodled a lot. Some of my doodles were first-person journals of made-up characters. One was an early *Jim's Journal* prototype, the others were prototypes of what later became my comic strip *Plebes*, which ran in *The Onion* for about seven years. The characters in *Plebes* were unflattering portraits of the kind of dopey college boys who wanted to be featured in the "Men of USC" calendar. The cartoon journal idea, on the other hand, was an outlet for little thoughts that I didn't have any other place to put.

I dropped out of college and reworked some of these first-person narrative strips and came up with *Jim's Journal*. I moved to Madison, Wisconsin, and brought my drawings to the University of Wisconsin school newspaper, *The Daily Cardinal*. The graphics editor liked them, but no one else did. He convinced the other editors to run *Jim's Journal* every other day. To almost everyone's surprise, including my own, the strip became quite popular on campus. They started running it daily. Then I started sending it out to other college newspapers. And it became quite popular on several other campuses as well. I also tried sending it out to the big newspaper syndicates. They, predictably, were not interested. Apparently, a comic strip that appealed to younger readers was of no interest to major daily newspapers.

After the strip had been running for a year or two, T-shirts based on *Jim's Journal* started selling from a local T-shirt shop, and then from other T-shirt shops. These shirts sold pretty well, and you still see them on people from time to time. But my contract with the T-shirt store ran out, and I decided I didn't want to sell Jim T-shirts anymore, so now you can't buy them anywhere.

Steve came over today.

"Hey, Mr. P," he said when he saw Mr. Peterson.

Then he said, "Jim, look what I brought."

It was the board game, Sorry.

We played a few games of Sorry, and Mr. Peterson kept pouncing on the game pieces.

Today Hal and I closed up the copy store at midnight.

When we were almost done, Hal said, "You can go home, Jim, I'll take care of the rest."

As I was walking away, I saw Hal through the window, wiping off the counters.

For a few seconds he concentrated his scrubbing in one little area, probably where there was a stain or something.

I was looking out my window today.

I saw a whole bunch of cars go by.

And some people.

Then Mr. Peterson jumped right in front of my face and I couldn't see anything.

Today Tony asked me if I wanted to play pool with him.

I said I would, and we walked over to the pool hall.

"I haven't played in a few weeks," Tony said, "But I still got the touch."

Then he hit the cue ball so hard it flew off the table.

Steve bought a new computer today.

"My old one was too slow on word processing," he said.

I watched him take it out of the styrofoam packaging and plug it in.

Once he had it hooked up, he played some sort of spaceship attack game.

I went over to Steve's place today to play on his new computer.

We decided to play Steve's favorite game, the one where you shoot spaceships.

Afterwords, we started talking about video games we used to play.

"There's no more good video games," Steve said. "They're all 'waste the drug dealer' now."

I was riding the bus today with Steve.

We were looking at some of the poster ads above the windows.

One was for a chiropractor who had a free consultation offer.

Steve said, "It's free, Jim. We should go," and I said okay.

I went to the chiropractor today because they had a free consultation offer.

The chiropractor asked me if I had back pain and I said not really.

"Good," he said. "It's never too early to start prevention."

And he showed me some exercises I could do so I would never have back pain.

I was hanging around with Tony today.

We got to talking about Steve and I mentioned that he just got a new computer.

"A computer?" Tony said, "How can he afford a computer when I can't even afford macaroni & cheese?"

I told him I guessed his parents gave him the money and he said, "I thought as much."

Today Tony said, "Hey, I got a great idea for a practical joke!"

He acted kind of secretive even though nobody was around who could have overheard us.

He said he figured out how to fool Steve into sending his computer away— by mailing him a fake recall notice.

He said, "This'll be the greatest hoax since my friend Dean threw water on me that one time."

Today I was watching TV with Ruth.

The channel wasn't coming in very well.

Ruth moved the antenna around.

"That's a little better, isn't it?" she said, even though it was just as bad.

Today Steve said, "Somebody's out to get me, Jim."

He showed me a letter he got in the mail today— a recall notice for his computer.

"When I called the company, they didn't know anything about it," he said.

"Also," he said, "the postmark is local, there's no model number, and some words are misspelled."

Today Tony chuckled and said, "I bet Steve's packing up his computer right this second.

I told him Steve got Tony's fake recall letter and knew right away that it was a fake.

"No way!" Tony said. "My plan was infallible!"

Then he shrugged and said, "oh well, it's Steve's loss. It could've been a classic prank."

Today Steve and I ran into Tony.

Steve asked Tony, "You wouldn't happen to know anything about a fake recall notice for my computer?"

Tony said, "Aw, you're no fun. That could've been a great prank."

Steve listed all the reasons it didn't work, and Tony got tired of listening.

Today I heard some loud banging noises out in the hall.

It was construction workers, doing some repairs on the apartment building.

(They were tearing out a wall and putting in a new one, it looked like.)

Mr. Peterson was scared to get close to the door because of all the noise.

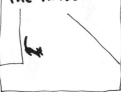

Today I woke up to the sound of hammering and wood planks banging around.

Mr. Peterson was at the foot of the bed, trying to sleep, but with her ears angled back.

Later, while I was brushing my teeth, I noticed the mirror shaking from all the pounding.

When I touched it, it made me vibrate, too.

Today the sound of a power saw woke me up.

I could also hear the workers in the hall laughing and talking.

I opened my door to look at them and they didn't notice me at all.

I fed Mr. Peterson and watched her bob her head while she ate.

Today I was eating some graham crackers when I heard the door buzzer.

It was the UPS person, who asked if I'd accept a package for somebody next door.

I said I'd accept it, and signed his clipboard.

Later, I took the package to the person next door and he said, "All right! I've been waiting for this."

Today Steve was saying he wished they'd make an Aquaman movie.

"He's my favorite super hero, and they haven't made a movie of him yet," he said.

He asked me if I'd go to an Aquaman movie and I said I suppose I would.

"See—," he said, "they should make one!"

I ran into Tony today and we ended up going to the post office together.

We stood in line and Tony was looking at the FBI posters of wanted fugitives.

He pointed to one and said, "Hey, this one looks like you, Jim."

Then he yelled to the postal workers, "I found one! I'll hold him down, you call the cops!" and laughed.

I worked with Dan at the copy store today. 	He was copying somebody's term paper or something. 	He showed me a spelling error he found on it and asked me if he should fix it. 	I said I didn't know what he should do. 
I had lunch with Dan today. 	We ate in the back of the copy shop. 	Dan ate an egg salad sandwich he brought to work with him. 	I ate a piece of pizza I got from the pizza place down the street. 
Today at the copy store Julie and I were just sitting around. 	It was a really slow day at the copy store. 	Julie sighed and said, "Did you see the game Saturday?" 	I didn't know what game she was talking about. 
Today Steve got a survey in the mail.	It was from some kind of marketing place and had a lot of questions on it. 	They wanted to know what kind of person Steve was and what he liked to buy. 	Steve asked if I'd help him come up with silly answers for it some time.

I ran into Steve today. 	He said he tried calling me last night but I didn't answer. 	I couldn't understand, because I never heard my phone ring last night. 	Steve said, "I figured you weren't home so I completely burglarized your place," he said, then chuckled. 
Today Steve, Dan and I filled out the marketing survey Steve got in the mail. 	Under race and religion and political opinion, Steve wanted to say he was an anarchist Catholic Eskimo. 	Dan thought he should be a New Age Republican from Iraq. 	He and Dan laughed and laughed, and couldn't decide which combination would be more fun. 
Steve, Dan and I wrote more silly answers on Steve's marketing survey today. 	Dan kept saying, "Tell 'em you make $5 a year—tell 'em $5 a year." 	Steve didn't want to, but Dan kept insisting on it, so Steve finally wrote it down. 	He also wrote that he has purchased 83 toasters in the last three months. 
Steve mailed his marketing survey today. 	He said, "I can't wait to see what kind of response I get." 	He said he thought maybe he'd get some free coupons or something. 	Afterwards, we played the space attack game on his computer and he beat me pretty bad. 

Today I went to a movie with Ruth and Steve.

It was a midnight showing of Pink Floyd: The Wall.

When it was over, Ruth said, "I didn't get it."

Steve tried to explain it to her, then realized he didn't get it either.

Last night Mr. Peterson was standing on my back, kneading me with her paws.

I was trying to fall asleep, but she was too distracting.

Finally she sat at my feet and fell asleep.

I must have, too, because that's the last thing I remember.

Today I was adding something up on my calculator.

I could barely see the numbers on the display.

So I held it under the light and the numbers showed up perfectly.

(I guess my calculator is the solar-powered kind.)

Today I went to the store to buy a loaf of bread.

I couldn't find the kind I normally get, so I got a different kind.

I took it home and ate some, and it was pretty good.

I decided to get this new kind from now on.

Today I ate lunch with Dan in the stock room. 	I noticed he brought some cookies with him that were jet black. 	I asked him why he was eating burnt cookies. 	He said, "I like things burnt... carbon adds flavor." 
I found a balloon today, just lying by the sidewalk. 	So I picked it up and took it home. 	Mr. Peterson liked playing with the string on it. 	She liked wrestling with the balloon too, and ran away in fear when it popped. 
I was really tired today and felt like sleeping in. 	But I had to get up to work at the copy store. 	When I got there, I told Joel I'd felt like sleeping in. 	He told me the same thing happened to him today. 
At the copy store today I worked with Julie. 	She had to re-arrange the little office supplies rack. 	I pointed out that she missed a roll of tape that was still out of order, and she threw it at me. 	But she wasn't really angry, she was just playing around, I'm pretty sure. 

Today I noticed Mr. Peterson flipping from side to side on the floor.

She looked at me, then flipped around some more.

I figured she was bored, so I tickled her belly and she grabbed my arm and play-bit it.

I rolled her around and she grabbed me and bit me some more.

Today Dan was talking about apes, comparing them to humans.

He was talking about their social structure and behavior.

"Human society is very similar," he said, "There's male hierarchy, posturing, everyone knows their place."

Then Hal came out of the back room and told us all to get back to work.

I was trying to write something down today, but my pen was out of ink.

I looked around for another pen, but couldn't find one.

I couldn't find a pencil or anything else either.

So I just wrote with the bad pen, hoping it would indent the paper enough to be readable.

There was some kind of storm or something today.

The sky was green and it was raining really hard and the wind was banging on the window.

Mr. Peterson was hiding under the big chair.

Then Steve knocked on the door, soaking wet, saying, "Nice day, huh?"

Today during my lunch break at the copy store, I got a taco.

I was going to eat it in the back room of the copy store, but the weather was nice, so I sat outside.

Then Dan came outside with his bagged lunch and ate with me.

He asked what I was eating, looked closely at it, and said, "oh, a taco."

I went over to Steve's place today.

He rented "48 Hours" and we watched it.

When it was over, I stayed there and we talked about this and that.

We talked about philosophical things and Steve said, "I don't think life is absurd or meaningless. I think it's funny."

Today Ruth and I sat and tossed popcorn to the ducks.

Ruth was telling me she liked the water.

"I've always liked lakes, boat rides, and all that," she said."

But she said it's been a long time since she's been on a boat, and she tried to recall when the last time was.

I was watching TV today.

There was nothing very interesting on, so I flipped around the channels.

At one point I saw the same coffee commercial on two different channels at once.

I eventually settled into an episode of Gilligan's Island that was pretty good.

Today at the copy store I ate lunch with Dan in the back room. 	He was eating a sandwich he brought from home. 	As he was taking a bite, the sandwich slipped out of his hands and landed on the floor. 	He looked down at it and said "I wish that hadn't happened." 
Today I worked at the copy store almost 9 hours. 	Joel was there and said he worked 9 hours today, too. 	Julie told us she remembered working 12 hours straight once. 	Then Hal said, "None of you have to take this job home with you— I do, and it's like working 24 hours a day."
"I did it, Jim," Tony said today. "I finally quit the shoe store."	"My brother thinks he fired me, but really I quit," he said. 	I asked him what he was going to do now. 	He said he didn't know, but that there was a whole world out there. 
Today I got a letter from my mom.	She told me all about things she's doing and people I haven't seen in a long time.	And she said one of her first piano students was giving a really important recital.	I thought of a lot of things I could write back and say, but when I sat down to write, I couldn't think of anything. 

Who Is Jim?

Jim is based loosely on my friend Chris Chan Lee, whom I met at USC. He was in film school and came out a cinematographer. He shot a few videos and a feature. Recently, when I made my independent feature film, *Spaceman*, he offered to be my cinematographer. Then he made his own indie feature, *Yellow*, but he got someone else to be his cinematographer.

Jim's cool demeanor and physical appearance came from Chris. Also, I'm pretty sure Chris's unkempt, too-short haircut was the inspiration behind Jim's spikey hair scribble.

Obviously I have been forced to draw on my own experience for Jim's day-to-day activities and thoughts. I tend to have more opinions than Jim, but there is certainly some Jim in me. When I'm in a calm mood, I'm a lot like Jim.

I learned about the philosophy of Taoism in Chinese history class at USC, and found the Taoists to be really interesting. They had a world view almost identical to mine, that of all my friends, and pretty much everyone my age. They were, in effect, slackers. While the Confucians were ambitious bureaucrats, the Taoists preferred to drop out of the rat race and just think about life. I purposefully gave Jim an overtly Taoist demeanor from the beginning. The cryptic, minimal tone of the *Tao Te Ching* was a big influence on Jim's language. However, I think the only reason his fourth-century Taoist personality resonated with a lot of college-age readers in the early 1990s is because of its striking similarity to the Generation-X milieu.

A few years after I had been drawing Jim, I discovered the fiction of Albert Camus. I found his plain sentences and characters' existential way of looking at the world to be frightfully similar to *Jim's Journal*, but he wasn't an influence, since I hadn't read his novels before.

Today Ruth came over and we ate some Cracker Jacks that she brought.

Ruth offered one to Mr. Peterson and she started to lick it.

Ruth laughed.

I told Ruth that Mr. Peterson likes to eat funny things sometimes.

Today Tony showed me his drivers license, which he had just gotten renewed.

"Don't I look like a dork?" he said, laughing.

He wanted to see my license, so I showed it to him.

"Ooh, you do not photograph well, Jim," he said.

Today I played some classical music on the radio.

Mr. Peterson slept on top of one of the speakers, like she sometimes does.

I was going to wash a load of clothes today.

But all the washing machines were being used.

Today I was just sitting around when I realized I was really tired.

So I took a nap.

I got up when Mr. Peterson knocked something off the table in the other room.

Today while I was watching TV, Mr. Peterson sat on my lap and purred.

I was watching some kind of loud car chase show, and the volume was turned way up.

But Mr. Peterson slept and purred despite all the noise.

Then, at one point, Mr. Peterson got up and shifted her position a little bit, then fell back to sleep.

Steve asked me to come to a baseball game today.

Steve isn't really a baseball fan or anything, but we decided it would be fun.

We sat and talked during the slow parts of the game.

Once, people started booing and Steve yelled. "Ya bum!"

I went out into the woods today.

I hiked around and looked at trees and stuff.

I tried to veer off the path once in a while, but the underbrush was too thick.

When I got home I plucked burrs and other things from my shoes.

I went to the store with Steve today to buy a candy bar.

The cashier said it was 53 cents, and I only had 50.

So she reached into her little penny box to get 3 pennies.

As we were leaving, Steve said, "They should have little boxes with $100 bills in them," and chuckled.

Today I was thinking of driving really fast.

It was like one of those video games where you drive a car.

I kept going faster and faster screeching around curves and oil slicks.

I wanted to keep going, but my imagination kept crashing the car.

I was feeling kind of bored today.

So I went to a cafe and ordered a chocolate sundae.

The woman who took my order seemed like she'd rather be doing something else.

When I was done eating the sundae I felt kind of sick.

Steve made a casserole today and invited Ruth and me over to eat it.

He said he was worried it might be too spicy and asked what we thought.

I said it maybe was too spicy and Ruth didn't say anything.

Steve kept saying "c'mon, Ruth, be honest," until she finally said, "It's a bit spicy but it's good."

I went over to Tony's place today.

He was trying to swat a fly, and said he'd been stalking it for 10 minutes.

Finally it landed on a wall, and Tony moved slowly toward it.

He swatted it as hard as he could, and said, "once again, man conquers beast!"

Smat!

I was reorganizing some books on my bookshelf today.

I made stacks on the floor and tried to put books on the shelf in some kind of order.

Mr. Peterson was sitting on the tallest stack, watching me.

It took me a long time because I kept stopping to read things.

Today I was over at Steve's place.

He showed me some 3-D glasses he still had from when he saw a 3-D movie a long time ago.

"I like 'em," he said. "Sometimes I wish I could just wear them like sunglasses."

But he said he wouldn't do that because people would think he was really weird.

Tony came by today to borrow some paper.

He said, "Hey, cat, how's it goin'?" when he saw Mr. Peterson.

I went into the other room to get some paper.

When I came out, I saw Tony having a moment with Mr. Peterson.

I sat at my desk today and did some word-find puzzles.

It was pretty dull, but I didn't have anything else better to do.

When I was little and did word-find puzzles, I always imagined the letters as giant towers.

And I had to find words by running around the edges of the letters to find the words.

| I was a little late for work at the copy store today.  | when I punched in, Hal said, "Running a little late, there, Jim?"  (He was flipping through account slips) | I told him I forgot I had to work until the last minute.  | He forced a smile and kept flipping through the slips.  |

| Today the sun was out, so Tony was sitting outside.  | He said, "Hey, Jim, could you do me a favor? I forgot my sunblock—here's my key."  | I went into Tony's room and found his sunblock in the bathroom. | I brought it out to him and he smiled at me and said, "Now if only I had some girl to rub it on for me." |

Today I threw a crumpled-up piece of paper into the trash, but it missed.

I was pretty close to the garbage can, and couldn't believe I missed.

I picked up the paper, tried a second time, and missed again.

I finally made it on the third try.

I was making copies all day today.

Joel kept bringing me more things to copy.

He asked me if I was sick of making copies yet, and I said almost.

He paused, then said, "Jim, that was the worst attempt at humor I've ever heard."

Today Tony and I played darts at one of his hangouts.

He complained about the plastic ribbed dart board because the darts didn't always stick in it.

Then he hit the bullseye with a dart, but it bounced right off. "That was in!" he said. "That was in!"

Then he asked if he could have the points for it anyway.

I made a big sandwich today and sat and read the newspaper while I ate.

Mr. Peterson jumped up on the table and walked across the newspaper, so I set her back on the floor.

She ran into the other room and I kept reading and eating.

Then she started meowing at the top of her voice and wouldn't stop.

meow — meow

Today Tony and I were walking around.

we came to a busy street and before I could react, Tony had run across.

He stood on the other side and waited for the rest of the cars to go by.

Then I crossed and we continued walking.

I bought a pop-sickle today.

It really hit the spot.

When I was done eating it, I put the pop-sickle stick in the trash.

And my fingers were all sticky.

Today Ruth called and said, "Hey, wanna do something?"

I asked her what she had in mind and she said, "How about a movie?"

We got together and looked in the paper and couldn't find any movies.

So we went to a play.

It was pretty good.

Today I scraped my hand on the corner of the window sill by accident.

It hurt pretty bad even though there was almost no mark.

I stared at my hand to see if I could see the microscopic throbbing.

I couldn't.

I decided to go over to Steve's house today.

When I got there I rang the buzzer but he didn't come to the door.

As I was leaving I saw Steve up in a tree, and he said, "Hi, Jim."

He told me he decided to climb a tree today because it would be fun.

Today I marked my calendar for some important thing or other.

But my pen ran out of ink because it was pointing upward.

I tried to angle the pen down so the ink would flow better.

But, doing that, my writing was so sloppy I could barely read it.

I was walking down the street today when I saw a mailman delivering mail.

He had huge stacks of mail in his truck and a big bundle in his hands.

I thought of how hard it'd be to keep track of all that mail all over the world.

And I just couldn't imagine how they do it.

I went out to eat with Steve and Tony today.

We all decided it would be kind of fun to get together.

Steve told us about a crazy cable TV ad he was watching the other day.

Tony was saying he's up for a really good tele-marketing job.

Last night I got up at 3am. or so with an important idea in my head.

I turned on the light by my desk and it practically blinded me.

I wrote down the idea on a little piece of scrap paper.

When I got up this morning and read it, I couldn't figure out what I'd thought was so important about it.

Today as I was leaving my apartment, Mr. Peterson trotted back and forth by the door.

In the hallway I noticed a roof access panel.

I climbed the little ladder up to it to see if it would open.

But it was painted shut.

Today Dan and I got off work at the same time.

We walked towards his place, which is on the way to mine.

He told me that he hopes time travel can be possible someday.

I asked him why and he said, "Just because it would be neat, don't you think?

Ruth brought me a present today.

It was a rustic-looking wooden laundry basket she got at the mall.

She got it because she's seen how the handles on my old plastic laundry basket are falling apart.

Mr. Peterson attacked the new basket and started biting off pieces of it.

Today Julie was telling me that she was looking for a better job than the copy store.

"I have a college degree," she said. "I shouldn't be doing this."

Then Hal gave us a whole bunch of copies to make.

Julie looked at what Hal gave us, almost as if to evaluate whether it was worth being copied.

Today I saw Julie at the copy store.

She wasn't working, so she didn't have her smock on.

She was making copies of her resumé so she could get a better job.

She looked closely at the copies to make sure they were perfect.

Today Mr. Peterson got a leaf somehow.

It must have come through the window when I had it open or something.

She was flipping over it and pouncing on it.

Then she carried it in her mouth and set it down in front of me.

I ran into Tony today.

He turned off his walkman and said, "Hey, Jim, what's up?"

I said, "Not much."

Then a guy on a unicycle went by and Tony said, "Get a loada that guy!"

I watched TV all last night.

There were a bunch of talk shows on.

Today when I got up I felt a lot more tired than usual.

I went to the corner store to get a newspaper and everybody seemed to be bustling.

I worked at the copy store from noon till 8 today.

When I got home I was really hungry.

I looked in the fridge to see if I had the makings of a sandwich.

Luckily, I found just the things I needed.

I went to the bookstore today and looked at the magazine rack.

I thought maybe I'd get a short story magazine or something.

I looked at the section with hot rod and wrestling magazines, too, just for fun.

A man walked in front of me and said, "Excuse me," and I stepped aside so he could get by.

I worked at the copy store today.

Hal came up behind me and watched me make copies.

I wondered if maybe I was doing something wrong.

Today I just sat and watched TV.

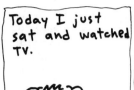

Steve came over for a while.

But then he left.

I don't think I realized he was there until after he left.

Today one of my kitchen drawers accidentally fell apart.

Mr. Peterson tried to eat the little bits of wood and cork that came off of it.

I nailed it back together and slid it back into place.

It works as good as new now.

Today I mailed a letter.

After I put it in, I opened the mailbox again.

My letter wasn't stuck to the side or anything, so I assumed it went in.

While the door was open, I decided to read when the collection times were.

Today I saw somebody who said he lost the little latch from his watch.

I helped him look for it.

"Found it!" he said, after a while.

Today I was throwing a crumpled-up piece of paper to Mr. Peterson.

she chased after it and pounced on it.

After a while she started batting it around herself, and I didn't need to throw it.

Then Ruth called and I described to her what Mr. Peterson was doing.

Today I went to a park.

I just sat on a bench.

Some people behind me were having a barbeque and I could smell the smoke from their grill.

Then two people on the path in front of me walked by saying, "mm—smells good!"

I was lying on my bed today, relaxing.

I was having trouble breathing because I was lying flat on my nose.

I didn't want to move my head though, because I was comfortable.

But eventually I had to move so that I could breathe.

Today I saw Tony shooting some baskets at the court near our building.

"I'm playing HORSE," he said. "Wanna play?" and I said sure, okay.

He said "Think fast!" and threw the ball at me.

I ducked to avoid being hit and it bounced into the street.

Today I was sitting at my desk when my light suddenly flickered off, then on again, with a soft clicking sound.

Mr. Peterson, who was sleeping at the foot of the bed, noticed it too, because she lifted her head up.

It didn't happen again, so I never figured out what caused it.

Mr. Peterson rested her head back on her hands.

Today I was sitting on my bed, staring at the ceiling.

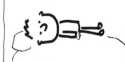

I saw a tiny black dot that I thought, for a second, was moving.

Then I saw Mr. Peterson looking intently at the same spot, making a chirping sound like a half-meow.

I decided the spot must be some sort of bug or something.

Today at the copy store it was really busy.

We had copying jobs stacked up on the counter and long lines of customers.

I gave somebody her copies and she said, "Wait, these aren't mine."

I looked through the stack until she pointed and said, "That's mine— the one right there."

Today I was washing my dishes after eating a sandwich.

A little drop of water flung right onto Mr. Peterson's head, and she shook her head and ran away.

When I finished the dishes I sat down and turned on the radio.

The speakers just popped really loudly— even with the volume all the way down.

Today Hal called me into his office and said, "Jim, you've been here almost two years, haven't you?"

I said I wasn't quite sure (I was looking at the pictures of his family on his desk.)

"Anyway," he said, "I figure it's time you got a 25¢ per hour raise."

After a few seconds he said, "Haven't you got any response to that, Jim?"

I was hanging around with Steve today.

I mentioned that Hal gave me a 25¢ per hour raise at the copy store.

He said he didn't think that added up to much over a week.

He figured out exactly how much it came out to, and it wasn't very much at all.

Ruth came over today.

We sat and ate popcorn and talked.

She was saying that she's always wanted to go to Europe.

"But I guess I wouldn't mind just learning one of the languages instead," she said.

Today Dan said I should come over to his place to watch a movie some time.

"I have a superb video collection," he said.

Joel, who was walking past us at the moment, chuckled to himself.

When Dan asked him what was so funny, Joel said it was nothing.

Today I went to Dan's place after work.

I couldn't believe how messy it was.

Dan said he had a really great video we could watch.

He said, "It's here somewhere," while sifting through clothes, garbage and stuff.

Today when I got to the copy store, Hal was talking to some police officers.

I went in back to punch in and found out from Julie that the copy store got robbed the night before.

"They stole some paper and messed up Hal's office," she said.

I looked at Hal and he was answering "no" and "not really" to a bunch of the officers' questions.

Today at the copy store, Hal was telling us what he thought of the copy store robbery.

"The police said it might've been a disgruntled former employee," he said, "but I doubt that."

Then Dan said, "They obviously tore up your office looking for money."

Then Joel looked at Dan and said, "Duh."

Today I was sitting down for a long time and my leg fell asleep.

I could barely make use of the leg, and walked around awkwardly.

Mr. Peterson looked at me with her eyes wide, like I was going to stomp on her.

The feeling eventually went away and I was able to walk just fine.

Today I was getting something out of the cupboard when a can of beans fell on my head.

It hurt really bad, and I went to the mirror to see if there was a mark or anything.

I couldn't see anything.

But I felt like there was a bump as big as a corn cob sticking out of my head.

Today Ruth came over and we just sat and talked.

I mentioned that I got hit in the head by a can of beans yesterday.

She winced and said, "ooh, that must have hurt."

I told her that it did.

Today Steve and I went over to Dan's place to watch The Godfather.

Dan had a whole bunch of papers, clothes and stuff on the couch that he threw onto the floor so we could sit.

Steve and Dan talked about the movie while we watched it because they'd seen it before.

They pointed out their favorite parts and got excited during the shoot-out parts.

I was watching TV today.

Mr. Peterson was sitting on my lap.

I watched an episode of Star Trek that I'd seen before.

Then there was some kind of talk show on that I eventually lost interest in.

Today I got up a little late and had to hurry to the copy store. 	When I got there, Hal was putting in an alarm system. 	The district manager of the copy store was there, too. 	They were standing around watching the guy from the alarm place install the alarm. 
I took my radio into the repair place today. 	The woman at the shop asked me what was wrong with it and I said the speakers popped even with the volume turned all the way down.	She put a tag on it and told me they'd call when it was fixed. 	(She had a little tuft of hair sticking straight out of her head that I couldn't help but notice.) 
Today when I got up, I realized I'd had a dream about today. 	I dreamt that I got up, went to work and everything else. 	Nothing weird happened in the dream, but now I thought I'd already lived through the day. 	So I felt like I was having to do it all over again.
Today I got up and fed Mr. Peterson, as usual. 	I made myself a bowl of cereal and read the newspaper while eating. 	I could hear Mr. Peterson chomping her food. 	I worked at the copy store till 8:30 and nothing very eventful happened. 

Today Steve came to the copy store and wanted me to make a copy for him.

(Hal was sorting the colored paper right behind me.)

When I gave Steve the copy, he asked, "So, you gonna give me this for free?"

Hal looked up and said, "You better not be giving out copies, Jim."

Today I was visiting Tony. (His apartment is on the top floor of the building.)

We looked out the emergency exit at the end of the hall.

Through the grate of the fire escape I could see the alley way, seven stories down.

Tony nudged me a little bit, yelling, "Watch out, Jim!" and it really startled me.

I made some brownies today.

I bought the brownie mix at the store the other day.

All I had to do was mix in an egg and some water, and bake them.

They tasted pretty good.

I got a free issue of Details magazine in the mail today.

They wanted me to subscribe, so they gave me an issue free.

I looked through it while I ate lunch (a left-over piece of pizza).

Mr. Peterson jumped on the table and sat right on top of the magazine.

Today Dan came over and we watched TV.

He looked through the TV schedule to see what was on.

We decided there was nothing interesting on, but we sat and watched it anyway.

The reception wasn't very good, so Dan adjusted the antennae every so often.

Tony came by today.

He told me he found a great job, "with five-fifty an hour plus commission!"

He said it was a telemarketing job.

He looked at the stuff on my table and said, "You get Details? No way!"

Today Ruth and I made some things out of paper maché.

Ruth mixed up a batch of it because she thought it would be fun.

She made a Viking helmet and I made a turtle.

Our hands got coated with the crusty goop.

I was throwing Mr. Peterson's ball around today when the phone rang.

It was somebody reading off a script, "Sir, don't you think cable TV is worth less than thirty cents a day?"

Then the person suddenly burst out laughing, and I recognized the voice as Tony.

"I thought I'd call and give you my spiel," he said. "Pretty good, huh?"

Today I was walking down the sidewalk when I slipped on some ice and fell.

People, standing on the other side of the street or wherever, stopped what they were doing and looked at me.

They didn't laugh or help or anything. They just looked.

I got up and continued walking.

Tony, Steve and I were hanging out today.

We were talking about which TV shows we liked, and Steve said The Simpsons.

"But I can't watch it at Jim's," he said, "because your reception is about as good as the moon's."

Then Tony said to me, "Cable TV is only like thirty cents a day," which is from his phone sales pitch.

I was watching TV today and the channel wasn't coming in very well.

I adjusted the antennae but it didn't help.

I remembered Dan saying I should put some tin foil on the antennae, so I tried that.

The reception was a little better after that.

I was walking with Tony today on his way to work.

"Hey, you should come in and meet some of the clowns I work with," he said.

I followed him into a big office filled with people talking on phones, and he pointed to an old guy smoking and said, "This is chuck."

Then Tony announced, "Hey, everybody, this is my buddy Jim," and a few people looked but nobody seemed interested.

Today at the copy store Julie and I were making a bunch of copies.

Our lunch break was just a few minutes away, but Julie said she wasn't hungry.

She asked. "What should I do on my break?"

I said I didn't know and she said, "Maybe I'll drop dead."

I was sitting in my chair today when Mr. Peterson started attacking my feet.

Then she looked at me, flipped over, then hid under the table.

The phone rang, and Mr. Peterson darted into the other room.

ring

It was the audio repair place saying my radio was fixed.

I went to the audio repair place today to pickup my radio.

While I was there, I asked if they sold antennaes, because mine was broken.

The woman working there asked me to describe the problem, so I explained my bad TV reception.

She said, "why don't you have cable?" and I said I didn't know.

Today I called the cable TV company.

"I think you're the last guy on earth without cable," Steve said yesterday.

I told the person on the phone I wanted to sign up for cable TV.

She put me on hold and I took the opportunity to unravel my phone cord.

Today the cable TV guy came. 	He had a big belt full of tools and hooked up my TV really fast. 

"Mind if I use your phone?" he said. I said sure and he dialed his number. 	While he was waiting for it to answer he pointed to Mr. Peterson and said, "Hey cat, how's it goin'?" 

I let Mr. Peterson outside today. 	She sniffed around by the stairs, like she usually does. 

A dog walked by and stared at her and stretched his leash to the limit. 	Mr. Peterson stared back, crouched down and froze solid. 

Tony came over today. 	"Whad'ya say I watch your TV for a while?" he said. 

I said okay. 	He plopped down on the couch and asked, "How's the cable TV workin' out for ya?" 

I worked at the copy store till closing today.	After we locked up, Hal said, "See you tomorrow, Jim. Have a good one." 

I walked home the long way, by the lake. 	When I got home, I sat and listened to a talk show on the radio until I fell asleep. 

Today Mr. Peterson and I saw the same dog we saw the other day.

This time he walked right up to Mr. Peterson.

She hissed at him and he walked away as if he wasn't interested anymore.

Mr. Peterson stayed in her cowering position for a few minutes after.

I rode the bus with Ruth today.

(She likes to take the bus sometimes instead of driving her car.)

We noticed that whenever another bus passed our bus, the two drivers always waved.

"I think that's nice," Ruth said.

Today I got home from the copy store around 4 p.m.

I was really tired, so I took a nap.

When I got up it was 6 o'clock.

For a second, I couldn't tell if it was morning or night.

Today Steve came over and said, "I'm bored."

We sat around for a while.

"I'm still bored," Steve said.

I Got Married

The fourth Jim book I did was *I Got Married if you can believe that*. While earlier I had thought Jim getting married would be too much of an event for so uneventful a comic strip, I realized nobody would keep buying my books if they all had titles like *I Made Some Brownies* or *I Didn't Do Much Today*. At some point, you have to accept the realities of the marketplace and select, at the very least, interesting titles. So, Jim got married. Well, in the daily comic strips that ran in newspapers Jim never got married. He and Ruth never lived together, and as for whether they were even a couple, I left that purposefully ambiguous. I tried to carry over some of that ambiguousness to the book, and explained it away by having Ruth read Jim's journal and get angry at him for only writing about tiny, unimportant things, and ignoring important events like their relationship. So, he only wrote about their wedding after she bugged him about it.

I got married at the age of twenty-two. Krista, whom I'd met at USC, moved back to Wisconsin with me. We went to the Justice of the Peace and signed a form. It was all very romantic.

Krista wanted to get a divorce after we'd been together for about nine years. That wasn't very romantic at all. So, we got divorced.

During our divorce was when I started the story line with Jim and Ruth ambiguously becoming a couple. Their marriage experience is not much like Krista's and mine. The odd coldness that would eventually creep into their relationship was meant to be a parody of the institution of marriage more than anything else.

After I got divorced, I didn't have too much positive to say about marriage. I still don't.

Today at the copy store I made copies while Julie worked the register.

Somebody came in and asked us to copy a magazine article he clipped out.

Julie said we can't copy it because of copyright laws and everything, which is store policy.

The guy just stood there for a while then Julie took the article and said, "Aw, heck, we'll copy it."

Today Ruth and I ate at a nice restaurant.

The waiter brought us some water and said he'd be right back.

He didn't come back for quite a while and Ruth said, "I wonder if he forgot about us."

But he eventually came and took our order.

Today Steve told me he really wanted a plant.

"I think it would brighten up my life considerably," he said.

So I told him he should probably go buy one.

But he said he didn't feel like getting up.

I decided to start reading a book today because I was bored.

The other day Steve loaned me a copy of Watership Down and said I should read it.

As I started reading, I noticed the glue on the binding was kind of old.

Then I noticed I could pull out all the pages with no effort.

Steve and I went to a greenhouse today.

They had hundreds of different kinds of plants, and we'd never even heard of most of them.

Steve really liked this one tree-type thing, but it was 350 dollars, not including the pot.

"you could buy a whole forest for that," he said.

Today Ruth and I went for a walk.

we passed by a cat in front of a house.

Ruth stopped to pet him and said, "Hi fella," and he seemed friendly.

I leaned down to pet him and he took off running, and Ruth said, "You scared him off, Jim!"

Today at the copy store Julie, Joel, Dan and I took our break at the same time.

We were all talking when Julie started telling a story about washing her smock.

Halfway through it, Joel started telling a different story and everybody turned to him.

Julie finished telling the story, mainly just mumbling it to me, since everybody else was listening to Joel.

Steve set up his new plant today.

He put it by the window so it could get enough sunlight.

we sat around and didn't say much about it.

Then Steve said, "Isn't this place, like, a hundred times more cheery?"

Today I worked eight hours at the copy store.

I was tired and looking forward to going home, plopping on my bed and reading more of Watership Down.

When I was unlocking my door I heard paper rustling inside.

I opened the door and saw that Mr. Peterson had strewn all the pages of Watership Down across the floor.

Today Hal made Dan and me scrub the lighted sign above the front door of the copy store.

We found a bird's nest up there.

Dan said, "It looks as though it's been abandoned for some time."

So he tossed it onto the sidewalk and it crumbled into bits.

Today Ruth and I went over to Steve's place.

She saw his new plant and said, "Oh, look, you got a plant."

Then she went off about how to water it, take care of it and everything.

Steve said, "Knowing me, it'll probably just die."

Today I was sitting at the table eating a sandwich.

Mr. Peterson jumped up on the table, looked at me, then walked up on my shoulders.

She got comfortable and just sat there for a while.

When I was done eating and started getting up, she jumped off and ran into the other room.

Today Tony said, "Six full glasses of water per day."	He said that's how much everybody is supposed to drink.	He filled up a glass, drank it, and said, "Delicious."	He set the glass down firmly and said, "That's number three."

Today Ruth and I went to a classical music recital.	The program said the were playing Brahms.	Ruth whispered, "I think it's important to expose yourself to culture, don't you?"	Then she started giggling at the conductor because he was flapping his arms like a lunatic.

Today Steve came over and sat in my chair.	I asked what he was up to and he just said, "Eh."	He said he was feeling kind of gloomy for no particular reason.	"Not enough water," Tony said.

I took Mr. Peterson outside today.	I scooped up some snow and showed it to her and she was afraid of it.	But after a while she was lying belly-up and feeling right at home.	When I brought her back inside, she was wide-eyed, darting back and forth, then stopping suddenly like she was possessed.

Today when I came home I saw the mailman putting mail in the apartment's mail boxes.

I stood there and waited for my mail.

He asked if I was expecting something important today and I said not really.

Today Tony told me the best way to get six glasses of water a day.

"Just always have a glass in your hand, and sip it throughout the day," he said

"Much better than chugging six entire glasses," he said. "Classier, too."

After he left, I noticed that he left his glass on top of my TV.

Ruth came over today.

Tony came by too, and told Ruth, "Are you getting your six glasses a day?"

Ruth smiled and said, "That's what they say, isn't it?"

Then she told Tony that tap water is fluoridated, which she knows because she's a dentist's assistant.

I went to the bookstore today to buy Watership Down.

(Steve loaned me a copy, but it was so worn out it fell apart.)

(And I got caught up in the story so I decided I should buy my own copy.)

I picked it off the shelf and a guy standing there said, "Rabbit book. Cool book."

Today I went to the video store with Ruth.

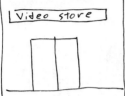

We didn't know what movie to rent, so we were looking around, trying to find one.

Every movie I wanted to get, Ruth wasn't interested in, and vice versa.

Eventually, we decided not to get anything, and went home.

Today Tony said to me, "Did you know fluoride is poisonous — and it's in our water!?"

I told him I guess I'd heard that.

"Why didn't you stop me when you saw me drinking it all the time?" he asked.

I said I didn't know and he pointed to me and said, "You'll stop at nothing to see me die."

Steve came over today.

He saw Watership Down sitting by my chair and said, "Hey, how do you like it?"

I told him I thought it was pretty good, and that the pages were falling out.

He sat down hard, exhaled loudly and said, out of the blue, "Wouldn't it be great to be, like, Eddie Murphy or somebody?"

Today Tony was making a hamburger and whistling a tune.

"Nothing like a whistled ditty to brighten your day." he said.

I told him that I've never been able to whistle.

"You freak!" he said.

Today Tony told Steve that I couldn't whistle.

Without responding, Steve put his fingers in his mouth and whistled really loud.

Then Tony did the same thing.

Today I was sitting around, trying to whistle.

I've never really been able to, so I was mostly just blowing out air.

But then a loud tooting sound came out, and Mr. Peterson jumped about two feet off the floor.

Then she looked at me like I was crazy.

It rained today, but really lightly.

At one point I couldn't tell if it was raining at all anymore, so I held out my hand to see.

Steve said he thought it had stopped.

But then he said, "Oh, I just felt a drop," so we knew it was still raining.

Today Mr. Peterson was rambunctious.

Steve said, "Don't you have any toys for this cat?"

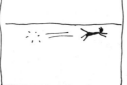

I realized I didn't, except for crumpled-up paper, which she likes.

"Mr. Peterson is deprived!" Steve said.

I decided to make Mr. Peterson a toy out of paper, which she likes to play with.

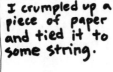

I crumpled up a piece of paper and tied it to some string.

Mr. Peterson seemed to like it, jumping up at it when I whipped it around.

Also today I worked the evening shift at the copy store and hardly anybody came in.

Today Mr. Peterson was grabbing at my shoelaces while I was walking.

I figured she wanted to play, so I got out her paper-on-a-string toy that I made.

She batted around at it for quite a while, then she got tired of it.

Later, I saw her flipped over by my shoes, chewing on my shoelaces.

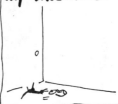

Ruth and I went to a garage sale today.

Ruth saw a Batman necklace and said, "Ha! Look at this."

We didn't end up buying anything.

As we left, Ruth said, "There were some neat little things there."

I went for a walk today and saw a dog.

For no reason, she came up to me and barked at me like crazy.

I wondered if there was something wrong with me that the dog could sense.

But after the dog left I realized I was probably okay.

Ruth wanted to go to Steve's today to look at his plant. 	"Oh, it's dying," she said. 	"I knew it would die," Steve said. "I have no luck with plants." 	Ruth tried to think of a way to save it, but couldn't think of anything. 
Today I got some stamps. 	I got the kind with "love" written on them with the picture of the puppy. 	The postal worker gave them to me and smiled. 	"Those stamps are cute, aren't they," he said. 
Today I was sitting around reading. 	I noticed Mr. Peterson sprawled out on the floor, bellied-up. 	She occasionally licked her hand, but pretty much stayed in the upside-down position. 	Then suddenly she jumped up and ran in the other room. 
Today I was walking around and saw a penny. 	I just walked past it without picking it up. 		Afterwards I was thinking it was weird to just pass up free money, even if it's just a penny. 

Today Hal asked me to work some extra hours next week.

I didn't really feel like it, but I said I would.

"Great," he said.

I'm not sure why I agreed to do it.

I had to get out my winter jacket today.

In a pocket I found an old grocery list.

One of the things on the list was horseradish sauce.

I couldn't remember ever needing horseradish sauce.

I was scratching Mr. Peterson's head today.

She liked it so much that she kept leaning back.

Finally, she fell over backwards.

Today Ruth came over with a bunch of leaves.

"I want to put them in a book," she said.

She said she used to like doing that when she was a little kid.

So she got wax paper and pressed the leaves and put them in a book and everything.

Tony called me really early this morning.

"Jim," he said. "My power went off! What time is it?"

I told him it was 5:30.

He thanked me and hung up.

Tony came by today to look through any newspapers I had.

"I'm cutting out coupons," he said. "Or should I say 'free money.'"

He told me he's already saved almost 3 dollars.

"It's all part of my goal to become a smart shopper," he said.

Ruth and I went to a coffeehouse she found today.

"Isn't this just the greatest place?" she said.

I thought it was okay.

"I think it's just great," she said.

I woke up this morning hungry for macaroni and cheese.

I thought about it all day at the copy store.

On my way home I bought some.

I cooked it and ate it and I think I waited too long because it didn't taste as good as I'd hoped.

Today Tony ran up to me and said, "Look what I got in the mail today!"

It was a little coupon book.

He stood there flipping through it for a second.

Then he asked if I'd gotten one in my mail and if he could have it.

Today at the copy store things were pretty slow.

Then for some reason a whole bunch of customers came in.

I worked really fast making all the copies.

After a while everything slowed down again.

Tony came over today, just as Ruth was leaving.

"Hi, Tony!" she said.

After she left, me and Tony just stood there.

Then Tony said, "why is she so damned happy all the time?"

Steve came over today.

He was holding his dead plant.

"I brought a toy for Mr. Peterson," he said.

He put it on the floor and Mr. Peterson sniffed it then walked away.

Today I worked the cash register at the copy store.

It was pretty busy.

After a while I ran out of one-dollar bills.

I told Hal and he said, "You need singles, huh?"

Today I was washing dishes.

Mr. Peterson was standing on the counter, watching.

When a little soap bubble floated past her, she just looked at it.

When it landed on the counter she watched it vanish then put her paw right on the spot where it landed.

Today I went to Ruth's to watch TV and eat pop corn.

The doorbell rang and Ruth said, "Who could that be?"

She got up to see who it was.

It was her friend, and they stood there and talked for half an hour.

Today at the copy store Hal interviewed somebody for a job.

Julie and I were working the counter.

"Another lamb to the slaughter," Julie said.

Then a customer walked up and she said, "May I help you?"

I went to the grocery store today to buy some cereal.

Tony came with.

As I was paying for my cereal, Tony lowered his head and exhaled.

Outside the store he said, "Jim, why didn't you tell me! I have a coupon for that cereal at home for a dollar off!"

Today Hal introduced me to a new employee.

"Her name is Erma," he said.

Then he took her around to see the rest of the store.

She pretty much just followed Hal around and didn't say much.

Today at the copy store Erma was making copies.

"You're getting the hang of things real quick," Hal told her.

Julie commented that Erma doesn't talk much.

"Hey, she's new," Hal said. "She'll loosen up in no time."

Today I was washing dishes.

Mr. Peterson was sitting on the counter, watching.

At one point she reached out her arm and tried to grab a plate I was holding.

I noticed it had some cheese residue on it.

Today at the copy store Erma couldn't figure out something on the big copier. 	Dan helped her. 	Then he came up to me at the counter. 	"Which do you think is the best Twilight Zone episode ever?" he asked. 
I went walking around with Tony today. 	We stopped at the store to get a snack. 	Tony said, "I think I have a coupon for oreos," and started digging through the coupons in his pocket. 	Two guys in line behind us started to snicker. 
Today when I came home I noticed Mr. Peterson was in the kitchen sink. 	As soon as I spotted her she jumped out and ran away. 	I looked in there and found a plate that she'd licked clean. 	I looked in the other room and saw her licking her hand and rubbing her face.
Tony came over today. 	I thought he'd be looking for more coupons, but he wasn't. 	"Coupons are dumb," he said. 	He turned on the TV and flipped through the channels. 

I walked over to Steve's today. 	His place was filled with boxes of envelopes and paper. 	"I'm helping my mom do some sort of mailing." he said. 	We sat around for a while and stuffed envelopes. 
I went over to Steve's again today. 	"We only have 7000 more envelopes to stuff," he said. 	We stuffed envelopes for a while, then played a game on his computer. 	"I don't mind taking a lot of breaks," Steve said, "especially since my mom doesn't have any deadline or anything. 
Today Ruth told me there was an old house she knew of that looks like a castle. 	She took me to go see it. 	When we got there it was dark and no lights were on in the house. 	"Ooh, scary," she said. 
When I came home today Mr Peterson was pacing by the door with her tail sticking up.	I patted her on the head and she rubbed up against my leg.	I sat down and relaxed and she ran back and forth across the apartment. 	

Today Tony and I stopped at a store for a candy bar.

Tony bought his candy bar and put a penny in the little penny box.

"Here's a little something for you," he told the cashier.

The cashier acted like he didn't even know Tony was there.

Today Steve and I walked by the part of the lake where people ice skate.

"Can you ice skate, Jim?" he asked.

I said I could, but wasn't very good at it or anything.

Steve said he hates all winter sports because they make your feet freeze off.

Tony came over today.

He opened the fridge to look for something to eat.

(He found a can of Pepsi.)

He sat down and said "I think you'd better check your fridge, Jim."

"It smells like something died in there."

Today I looked in my fridge to see if I could find what Tony smelled.

I could sort of smell it, but it wasn't very strong.

I looked way in back and found a leftover container of something I'd forgotten about.

I just threw away the food, the container, and everything.

Ruth came over today.

She brought a present.

At first I thought it was for me, but she said, "It's for Mr. Peterson."

"It's a cat hair brush," she said.

I ran into Mike today.

I used to work with him at McDonald's.

He said he was a stand-up comedian now.

He said he hates when he tells people that because "they always say, 'oh, tell me a joke!'"

Yesterday Ruth told me that it's a good idea to brush cats.

That's why she got me a brush for Mr. Peterson.

I brushed her and she flipped over and exposed her belly.

When I was done she followed me around.

Today Steve and I saw a movie.

When it was over I got up to leave.

But Steve didn't get up, so I sat back down.

(Steve likes to stay for the credits.)

Today I went to buy some soap, then went to work at the copy store.

Dan was working there too.

I realized I hadn't worked with Dan in quite a while.

Just as I was thinking that he said, "I haven't worked with you in quite a while, Jim."

Steve came over today.

I told him I ran into Mike and that he's a stand up comedian now.

"Everybody's a stand-up comedian now," steve said.

"Hey—new soap!" he said.

Today Steve and I went to see Mike perform his stand-up routine.

Comedy Club

It was a small club, and there were hardly any people there.

Mike was the third or fourth comedian to perform, and steve and I thought he was pretty funny.

He came to sit with us afterwards and said, "Not exactly the Tonight show, but hey."

Today Tony was telling me how cold his feet were.

I noticed he was barefoot, so I suggested he get some slippers.

"Slippers are for sissies," he said.

But he eventually decided slippers weren't such a bad idea.

I washed a load of clothes today.

I sat around and waited while they were in the dryer.

When the machine was done, I checked the clothes and noticed my big towel was still a little damp.

So I ran the dryer a little bit longer.

Today I went to Tony's place.

He was watching a nature documentary on TV.

I thought maybe he was just flipping around the channels, but he wasn't.

After a while he said, "Penguins are amazing!"

We got a fancy new color copier at the copy store today.

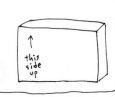

this side up

Hal helped the delivery people set it up.

Julie added color copies to our price sign.

COLOR   75

"It's the dawning of a new era," Hal said.

Today I was sitting around with Steve when we heard a knock on the door.

It was Tony, and he was wearing big silly moose slippers.

Steve laughed out loud, but Tony wasn't laughing.

"I told my mom I needed some slippers," he said, "and look what she sent me!"

Today Tony called and said I had to come over right away.

So I did.

When I got there, Tony said, "Close your eyes, I've got a surprise."

While my eyes were closed I heard a dog panting and barking.

"You were supposed to be quiet you mutt!" he said. Then he told me the dog was the surprise.

Today Tony told me he was taking care of his brother's dog while he was away.

"He went to Canada," he said.

Tony was throwing around a little bone for the dog.

The dog would go after it really fast then bring it back to Tony, wagging his tail like crazy.

"Dogs are great," Tony said.

Today Steve and I went over to see Tony's dog and Steve asked, "What's his name?"

Tony told us his name was "Dog" and showed us how he fetches.

Dog ran after his bone into the other room, and we heard something big fall over and break.

"Dog, no!" Tony yelled.

I usually feed Mr. Peterson first thing in the morning.

But today when I got up I noticed I was out of cat food.

So I had to walk to the store and get some.

By the time I got back it seemed like Mr. Peterson wasn't interested in eating anymore.

Today at the copy store Dan came up to me in the back room. 	He said he wanted my advice on something. 	"How should I begin a courtship of someone?" he asked. 	I told him I didn't have any idea. 
Today Tony came by with his dog. 	"I thought I'd introduce Dog to Mr. Peterson," he said. 	We looked for Mr. Peterson but couldn't find her. 	Eventually we noticed she was hiding under the bed. 
Last night I was sitting in bed reading my book. 	Suddenly I felt like I was flying. 	I stopped reading the book so I could feel the sensation better. 	Then it stopped, and I went back to reading my book. 
Today Ruth and I were out walking when we ran into Tony. 	Ruth said, "oh, look at the cute puppy!" and pet him. 	Tony said, "Having a dog is a pain." 	"You have to walk the damned things constantly," he said. 

Tony's brother came back from his trip today.

So Tony gave him his dog back.

(Tony was taking care of the dog while his brother was away.)

"Having a dog is a hassle," he said. "What I really want is my own children."

At the copy store today Dan was carefully examining two sheets of paper.

He said one was twenty-pound stock and the other was sixty pound.

"I'm trying to figure out exactly what makes them different," he said.

Then Hal came out from the back and yelled, "Get the hell back to work!"

Today when I got up Mr. Peterson was standing on my chest, looking right at me.

As soon as I opened my eyes she let out a big meow and ran into the kitchen.

(That's because she knows she gets fed when I get up.)

After I fed her I looked out the window and saw that it was raining really hard.

Today I accidentally broke a bowl.

It smashed against the sink as I was washing it.

It was a ceramic bowl that was microwave-safe and it was the only one I had.

Little slivers of it flew every where and I tried to pick up every last one of them.

Today I went to the store to buy a bowl.

I picked one out and asked the cashier if it was microwave-safe.

She said it should say on the bottom, then tittered and said, "Oh—our price tag covers it up!"

So she took a few seconds to pick off the price tag, which was the kind that doesn't come off very easily.

Today I was walking down the street when I saw a guy fixing his bike.

"Hey, could you gimme a hand here?" he said.

I held a wrench while he tightened a screw.

He thanked me, then described how he almost got in an accident a few minutes ago, which is why he stopped to look over his bike.

Today Steve told me he was going to be on the local TV news.

He said he was shopping at the grocery store when the news crew was asking people questions.

I asked him what for and he said they just wanted his opinion about some food-related news story.

"But that doesn't matter," he said. "What matters is I'm gonna be on TV."

Steve was on the local TV news today and we all went to his place to watch.

They did a few national news stories, then they did the story Steve was in.

He was in the grocery store and they asked what he thought about a certain issue and he gave his opinion.

We all clapped and cheered, and Steve bowed. Tony said, "You were hardly on two seconds!"

Today I got up and fed Mr. Peterson.

When she was done eating she started washing her head.

She licked her hand then rubbed it on the side of her face a few times.

One time she caused her ear to flip inside-out, and it stayed that way until she rubbed it again and it popped back to its normal position.

Today I was calling somebody when Mr. Peterson jumped up on the counter.

She walked right in front of the phone, so I couldn't dial the number.

I paused while waiting for her to move, but she just stood there looking at me.

I put her on the floor and started dialing again, but she jumped up and stood in the same place.

Today Tony told me to watch the local news tonight because he was on it.

"I was right on camera, Jim—right on camera," he said.

He said he was walking by the lake when they were doing a story on it or something.

I watched the channel he told me to watch, but I didn't see him on it.

I saw Tony today and told him I watched for him on the news last night but didn't see him.

"Yeah I know," he said. "They must have cut me out."

"'Cause I was right on camera, Jim—right on camera."

Then he said, "I guess my public will have to wait for my next big appearance."

Today I came home from work around 9 p.m.

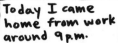

I hung my coat on the door knob without paying attention and it fell on the floor.

I ate, then watched TV for a couple of hours.

I walked past my coat and saw Mr. Peterson sound asleep on it.

I was sitting around today when I thought cookies would taste really good.

So I went to the store to buy some.

The kind I normally get, Keebler Soft Batch chocolate-chip, were sold out, so I settled for chocolate-chip walnut.

They weren't so bad.

Today I came home and hung my coat on the door knob.

Then I cooked up a bowl of soup.

I heard a repetitive scraping sound coming from the front door, then it stopped.

I went to see what it was and saw Mr. Peterson lying on my coat, which I guess she yanked off the door knob.

Today I was looking out my window.

I was just passing the time.

I would pick a certain person and follow them as long as I could see them.

One person came from inside a building next to mine, then kept walking up the street until all I could see was a speck.

I went over to Ruth's place today. 	She was just sitting around reading a book. 	I asked her what book she was reading and she told me.  (It was a mystery novel.)	Then she got into explaining the plot and I wasn't interested anymore. 
I went outside to read my book today. 	But it was too cold to be reading outside, so I came back home. 	Once I got home, I didn't feel like reading anymore. 	And there was nothing on TV either. 
I was sitting around today watching TV. 	Suddenly I remembered I was supposed to work at the copy store. 	I hurriedly grabbed my coat, but I didn't notice Mr. Peterson fast asleep on it. 	She got flipped, landed on her side, and ran into the other room. 
I brushed my teeth this morning, like any morning. 	First, I squeezed some toothpaste onto my brush. 	Then, before I got any further, my toothpaste fell off my brush into the sink.	So I squeezed on some more. 

Today when I was walking home from the copy store I saw a baby mouse in an alley.

He was sitting in the middle of the alley like he didn't have the sense to hide.

He was really young. It looked like his eyes weren't even open yet.

I could see his little ribs expand as he breathed.

On my way to the copy store today I went through the alley.

The baby mouse was still there and I leaned in to get a closer look at him.

He must have heard me because he hobbled as fast as he could about five feet, then stopped to catch his breath.

I got some bread crumbs and put them next to him, but he didn't eat them.

Today I was lying in bed trying to fall asleep.

I kept thinking about the baby mouse, wondering why he got abandoned and whether he'd make it.

Mr. Peterson was sitting on the window sill, then suddenly whipped around, trying to catch her tail.

I knew that if Mr. Peterson saw that baby mouse she'd bat him around until he was dead.

On my way to the copy store today I stopped by the alley to see the baby mouse.

He was out in the open, in the middle of the alley.

When I got closer, I could see that he was dead, just lying there, bellied-up.

When I came into the copy store, Joel and everybody were laughing at a joke, but I couldn't help feeling sorry for that mouse.

Today Ruth told me her brother was getting married. 	She said she's supposed to be a bridesmaid in the wedding. 	"I love weddings," she said, "except when I'm in 'em." 	She asked if I wanted to come and I said okay. 
Today Ruth took me out to buy a suit for her brother's wedding. 	I tried on some suits and felt pretty awkward wearing them. 	We eventually picked one, even though I felt just as awkward in it as all the others. 	The clerk helping us said to me, "You don't dress up much, do you?" and I said no. 
Today Ruth and I drove to her brother's wedding. 	We got there and Ruth hugged all her relatives while I just stood there. 	The ceremony was quick, and I think I noticed Ruth holding back a tear. 	At the reception afterwards a guy said to me, "I give 'em two years tops." 
Today there was a knock on my door. 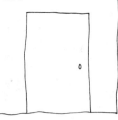	I said, "come in," but nobody came in. 	I opened the door and saw Tony on crutches. 	"Behold the gimp!" he said. 

Who Are Tony, Steve, Ruth, and Mr. Peterson?

People always want to know if the characters in *Jim's Journal* are based on real people. Most of them aren't. The few characters who were inspired by actual people have long since taken on lives and personalities of their own, and I no longer associate them with their real-world inspirations.

Tony was originally inspired by one of the photographers at *The Daily Cardinal*. I don't remember his name. He was a talkative guy who had been there a while, and talked to me like he was a veteran and I was a novice, which was pretty much the case. Nonetheless, I liked the way his bumpy hair looked and I found the dynamic between us to be amusing. I thought he'd make a good foil for Jim. And I thought Tony was a good name for such a character.

Steve is harder to peg. I don't know where he came from, exactly. Physically, he might have come partly from Mark Leonard, who was one of my best friends in high school. Mark and I used to talk about comedy theory all the time. He was really funny and I always thought he would find a way to make a living being funny. I think he ended up working for the state or doing some kind of insurance thing (which, come to think of it, is pretty funny). I thought Steve, on the other hand, would be a more useful character in Jim's universe if he thought he was funny, understood a lot about humor theory, yet wasn't the least bit funny himself. Another layer of anti-humor, I suppose.

Ruth is a construct with no real-world influence. If anything, she is inspired by the character of Boots in James Sturm's hilarious *Down and Out Dawg* comic, which ran in *The Daily Cardinal* back in the day. Boots was the very large cat girlfriend of Dawg. I thought Jim should have a very large girlfriend, too. I also may have borrowed a little of Ruth's chirpy personality and a bit of her hairstyle from a girl I met on the first bus out of town when I left home at the age of eighteen.

Mr. Peterson is an aggregate of some of my cats, at first Yule, then mostly Felix. Felix always has a lot to say, and he doesn't so much meow as bleep. Also, he's a girl cat, but I've always referred to him as a he. Why, I don't know. Maybe it's because he's neutered and pretty much genderless. Furthermore, he doesn't mind what I call him. Felix is black and white, but I wanted Mr. Peterson to be just a black blob with a barely recognizable cat form—sort of a parody of the calculatedly cuddly cats in most comic strips. However, I wanted him to transcend the anti-humor and actually be cute and cuddly, despite the fact that he was just a scribble. Berke Breathed's not-very-cuddly Bill the Cat from *Bloom County* was the same sort of cartoon-cat parody, but was pure anti-humor, not anti-anti-humor like Mr. Peterson.

Felix, by the way, is getting on in years now (he's ten as of this writing), but still bleeping.

Yesterday Tony came by on crutches.

He told me he tore some ligaments in his ankle trying to dunk a basketball.

Today he asked me to fix him a bucket of ice because he couldn't carry it in his condition.

He stuck his foot in the ice and winced. Then he said, "Now can you bring me a sandwich?"

Today I was sitting around at home when Tony called.

I went to his place and he asked me to make him some food.

"It hurts just to stand up, Jim, I swear," he said.

I made him a sandwich and while he ate it he said, "My complements, Jim. The perfect amount of Miracle Whip."

I went over to Mike's today to see what he was up to.

He was sitting with a cast on his leg and with crutches next to him.

He said in a silly dramatic voice, "Leave me—I cannot face you as half a man!"

Then he said he was just kidding and to just come right in.

I told Steve today that both Tony and Mike hurt themselves and were on crutches.

We couldn't believe the coincidence.

"Just watch," he said. "Next, I'll break a leg, or you will."

I said yeah and laughed along with him, even though I didn't really think that would happen.

I was walking around outside with Steve today.

We passed by some people juggling on the grass.

We sat and watched them for a while.

"They're pretty good," Steve said.

Steve and Ruth came over today to watch a movie on cable.

It was Under Siege.

We watched it and ate popcorn that Ruth brought.

When it was over we turned off the TV, sat around and didn't say much of anything.

Today Mike and I were hanging out together.

Mike had to go to the comedy club tonight and he was thinking up new material.

"I'm actually glad this happened to my knee," he said. "because now I can joke about it."

"For once I can stop using the silly fat-guy gimmick," he said.

Today Mike came over and we just sat around.

As he was leaving Tony came over.

They had trouble maneuvering through the door with their crutches.

We all thought it was kind of funny.

I went over to Steve's place today.

"Watch this, Jim," he said. "watch this."

Then he juggled for about two seconds until he lost control of all the balls.

"Pretty good, huh?" he said.

Today Tony came over on his crutches.

He set them by the door and said, "check this out, Jim."

He took a few cautious steps, yelling, "It's a miracle! It's a miracle!"

(He explained that part of his rehabilitation was to walk and stuff.)

Ruth and I went to see Mike perform at the comedy club today.

He made up a funny story about how he broke his knee fighting Black Belt Jones.

(He actually fell over a guard rail in the parking lot.)

When he was done he sat with us and Ruth said to me, "Isn't it neat that we know someone famous?"

Today Ruth and I went to see her friend Susan.

She had just had a baby, which she named Alice, and we held her.

She was very small.

"She's so small," Ruth said.

Today I got up early. 	I worked at the copy store from 10 a.m. till 4 p.m. 	I worked with Joel, who at one point said, "This place is nowhere, man." 	Then I went home and Mr. Peterson, who was napping on the chair arm, looked up at me for a second or two, then went back to sleep. 
I called some company today and they put me on hold for a long time. 	I just sat there and listened to the Muzak. 	I heard renditions of "You Are So Beautiful," and a Billy Joel song that I don't know the name of. 	When the next available representative finally answered, I forgot all about the music. 
When I got up today the floor was cold. 	So I put on some socks. 	Later in the day I told Tony about the cold floor. 	He gave me the pair of silly moose slippers his mom gave him. 
Today when I got up the floor was cold. 	I put on Tony's silly moose slippers. 	They were warm. 	As I walked, Mr. Peterson batted at the little foam antlers that stick out.

Today after I got up I ate a bowl of cereal.

I didn't have anything to read or look at while I ate, so I stared at the cereal box.

In small printing on the side of the box was a toll-free number I could call if I had any questions about the cereal.

I stared at it during almost the entire time I ate and couldn't think of any questions I would ask.

Today I got up a little late, and was supposed to work at the copy store.

I fed Mr. Peterson.

Then I ate a banana and an english muffin while getting dressed.

I got outside and was surprised to see that it had snowed quite a bit.

Today I went to Ruth's place and she answered the door slumped over in her bath robe.

"I have a cold," she said.

She also said she didn't know if it would be a good idea to visit her.

"You don't want this cold," she said.

Today Ruth called me and asked if I'd pick up some cold medicine for her.

I said I would and headed out to the store.

They didn't have the kind she wanted, so I got a different brand.

I showed up at her place and explained that they were out of the kind she wanted and she said, "whatever."

Today Ruth was telling me about a bad dream she had. 	She was working at the dentist's office, like she normally does. 	Except her dentist was frankenstein's monster. 	"It was so scary I woke up in the middle of the night screaming," she said. 
Ruth is finally getting over her cold. 	"I'm so happy it's over with," she said. 	Then she noticed that she was all out of Kleenexes. 	She flattened the box and put it in the trash. 
Today I was walking home from work after dark. 	I noticed it was a clear night and you could see all the stars. 	I decided to lie in the snow and stare up at the sky for a while. 	I started to get sleepy and felt like I didn't have the energy to get up. 
Ruth said today that my apartment could use some cleaning. 	"I don't mean to sound rude," she said, "but men are slobs." 	She said she'd help me clean, and that it would be no big deal. 	We started by vacuuming and dusting. (Ruth vacuumed and I dusted.) 

I finished cleaning my apartment today.

I scrubbed the bathroom and the kitchen and everything.

I even scrubbed out the kitchen cabinets.

when I was done, I had a lot of energy left, but I took a nap anyway.

Today was trash day.

I got out a big plastic garbage bag to fill it with all my trash.

I tried to open it, but it wouldn't open.

I realized I was trying to open the wrong end, so I tried the other end and it opened right up.

Today I went to the grocery store to buy a whole bunch of food.

I got milk, bread, frozen peas, apples, hot dogs and some macaroni & cheese.

While I put all the food away, Mr. Peterson jumped in the bag and stayed there for a long time.

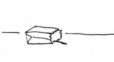

I cooked up some macaroni & cheese with chopped-up hot dogs in it and watched TV.

Today I was just sitting around watching TV.

Tony came over and said, "Hey, Jim, how's it goin'?"

We sat and watched TV for a while.

He started sniffing and said, "Did you clean or something?"

Ruth came over to visit today. 	we were just sitting around when we noticed Mr. Peterson sneezing. 	Ruth reached out to her and said, "God bless you, Mr. Peterson." 	Mr. Peterson ran away as fast as she could.
Steve and I were walking around today when we heard a funny squeaking noise. 	It was coming from a squirrel who was sitting next to a dumpster. 	We noticed he was looking up at another squirrel who was eating an english muffin wrapper. 	Steve said, "It would appear the one below wants the other one's english muffin wrapper." 
It was really cold outside today. 	I stayed inside and read a book. 	Mr. Peterson sat right under my light, so I couldn't see. 	I moved her out of the way and she squawked at me and went right back under the light. 
Today Ruth and I went out to eat. 	"This place is pretty good," she said. 	I went into the bathroom, where somebody had etched something on the wall. 	"This place sucks!" it said. 

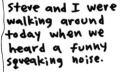

Today Tony popped his head in the door.

He said. "Jim!" Then he said "Wait, hold on."

Then he was talking to somebody in the hall.

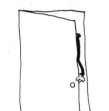

Then he just closed the door and didn't come back.

Today I was planning to do my laundry.

But I noticed I didn't have any quarters.

I went to the bank to get some.

The teller gave me the quarters and said, "Doin' laundry?"

Tony came over today.

"Do you have a set of luggage, Jim?" he asked.

I said not really.

"I should get me one," he said.

Today as I was leaving my apartment I noticed a cat in the hall.

Before I knew it Mr. Peterson bolted out the door toward the other cat.

They just stood in front of each other for a second.

Then the other one hissed and Mr. Peterson hightailed it back inside.

Today I went to the store with Tony to buy some luggage.

"I think everybody should own a quality set of luggage," he said.

The salesperson showed us the lowest-priced set, which cost $500, and Tony said, "Alright, thanks anyway."

As we were leaving, Tony said, "Can you believe that place? 500 bucks for suitcases!"

Today after working at the copy store I came home and sat down.

Mr. Peterson came out of the bedroom, groggy-looking.

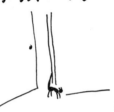

She did a big stretch, then walked over to me.

She jumped on my lap and folded her hands in.

Today Steve and I went bowling.

We were no good at it, so we didn't play for very long.

As we were handing in our shoes, Steve told me he was going on a trip.

I asked him where and he said, "To visit my grandparents. wanna come with?"

Today Steve and I drove to the small town where his grandparents live.

We stopped at a gas station on the highway.

We looked over the food and stuff to get something for the road.

"Not the best selection of snack cakes I've ever seen," Steve said.

Steve and I arrived at his grandparents' house today.

Steve's grandma said, "Oh good. Two strong boys. I could use some help in the yard."

So we spent the day hauling some bricks in her back yard.

Steve's grandpa woke up from a nap, came outside and said, "Is that young Steve?"

Today Steve and I explored the town where his grandparents live.

It's pretty small— only about one thousand people, Steve's grandpa said.

We went down to the pond by their house and saw a white rabbit.

We went to a Dairy Queen-type place and the guy said, "You in town for the Polka Fest?"

Today Steve and I helped his grandpa down in his basement workshop.

He was sawing up wood to build a birdhouse.

He held up a piece and said, "Look at that wood. Only the good lord can make something so beautiful."

My job was to grab the scrap wood off the table saw and throw it in the bin.

Today I got up and ate some pancakes that Steve's grandma made.

She patted his grandpa and said, "Grandpa just loves his pancakes."

After we ate, we hung up Grandpa's birdhouse and sat on the porch.

"I think that house will be a big hit in the spring," Steve's grandma said.

Steve and I drove back home today.	While we were driving, we saw a sign that said, "Treever, population 140."	Steve said, "Hey, let's get jobs at the cafe in Treever and live there."	He sort of chuckled then said, "Could you imagine that?"

When I got home yesterday, Mr. Peterson was eating a kleenex.	I took it away from her and she ran around the apartment for a while.	Ruth, who took care of Mr. Peterson while I was gone, left a note.	It had an account of the past few day's events, and said, "I think Mr. Peterson misses you!"

Today I got a bunch of junk mail.	I threw it on the floor and Mr. Peterson tried to burrow in it.		But she got tired of it after a while.

Today Ruth and I played a game of miniature Battleship.	(Her sister got it for her as a gift.)	At the end of the game I located her biggest ship.	When I did, she said, "You sunk my battleship!" and laughed.

Today was a pretty cold day.

I came inside and took off my coat and grabbed a kleenex.

A new kleenex automatically popped out of the box when I grabbed one.

I examined the box to see if I could figure out how it worked.

Today I was just lying around doing nothing.

Then Steve called and said he'd be right over with some incredible news.

Before he came over, I fixed myself a sandwich and ate it.

He came over and told me he was the lucky winner of a ten dollar shopping spree at the grocery store.

Today I went with Steve to help spend his ten dollar shopping spree.

He was explaining how he registered for it by dropping his name in a box at the store.

"I used to think nobody ever won those things." he said.

We arrived at the store and they didn't even give him a shopping spree. They just handed him a ten dollar bill.

I worked at the copy store today.

Julie told me that today was her birthday.

I wished her a happy birthday.

"Oh, shut up," she said.

Today at the copy store, Steve came in.

He asked if he could use the self-serve copier and I said sure.

After he made his copies, he came back to the check-out counter.

He asked me, "How can you stand working here?"

I went to the store with Tony today.

We were looking at the magazine rack.

"I should subscribe to more magazines," he said. "You know, to keep informed."

Then he picked up some tattoo-biker magazine and said, "You should get this one, Jim."

Today Tony was reading Rolling Stone magazine, which he bought the other day.

"You'll never guess how much Janet Jackson makes in a year," he said.

I said I didn't have any idea.

"A lot," he said.

Tony came over today and said, "I've decided how I'm gonna make my millions, Jim."

"Writing songs!" he shouted.

He said big-name recording artists are always looking for good new material.

Then he asked if I had any ideas for a song.

Last night I was sitting in bed staring at the ceiling.	I wasn't tired, so I just sat there.	I felt Mr. Peterson jump up on the bed and walk up my legs.	Then she came up to my face and I could feel her cold, wet nose touch my face. 
Today some people were painting the inside of Ruth's apartment. 	Ruth made polite conversation with the painters, but they didn't seem to want to talk. 	They brought a radio, which they had tuned to the rock station. 	So Ruth decided we should leave them alone, and we walked around outside even though it was kind of cold. 
Today Ruth and I went to Steve's place. 	Ruth's apartment was still being painted, and she just needed some place to go. 	We played some of Steve's computer games. 	Ruth played along and had a good time even though she kept saying she was no good at video games. 
Ruth and I watched the local TV news for a while today. 	Mr. Peterson was trying to burrow into Ruth's new coat, which was on the big chair.	A report on the news told about somebody who got shot. 	Ruth said, "Wouldn't it just be terrible to be shot like that?" 

Today Mr. Peterson was sleeping on top of my backpack, which was on top of the table.

I didn't notice at first, but she was pretty far off the edge of the table.

Suddenly the backpack fell and Mr. Peterson fell off the table with it.

She ran across the room and shook her head so hard I could hear her ears flapping.

Today at the copy store Julie was carrying a big box of paper.

She had to walk through the narrow passage where I was standing.

So she headed straight for me and said, "Move. Move. Move."

I got out of the way and she walked right by.

Today Steve and I were watching TV.

We watched the Star Trek episode where Data learns to be funny.

When it was over, Steve asked me, "Jim, do you think I'm a funny guy?"

I said I guess so.

Today Steve told me he's been talking to Mike about working together.

He said they thought of a funny TV sitcom idea.

"It would be set in Hell," he said.

He said they were thinking of writing a script for the pilot episode.

Today Steve and I went over to Mike's.

They were planning to write a TV sitcom that takes place in Hell.

"Hey," Mike said, "Let's call it 'Hell in a Handbasket.'"

Steve laughed and said, "Perfect!"

I went over to Mike's place today.

He and Steve were there to write a TV script.

But we mostly just sat around talking.

"What I'd really like to write is a super-hero movie," Steve said.

I ran into Steve today.

I asked him how his TV script writing was coming along.

"I don't know," he said, "we haven't done much on it."

Then he yelled, "Look out!" just as a guy on a bicycle came barreling down the sidewalk.

I ran into Mark today.

He was in creative writing class with me a long time ago.

He asked what was up and I told him a couple of my friends were writing a TV sitcom script.

"TV is a vast wasteland," he said.

I decided to start reading a book today.

It's The Sirens of Titan, by kurt Vonnegut.

So far, it's a pretty good book.

Tony and I played basketball today.

He knew of a park near by that had a basketball court.

We didn't play a real game or anything. We just leisurely shot some baskets.

Every time Tony made a basket without hitting the rim, he'd say, "Nuthin' but net!"

Tony and I played basketball again today.

Today we decided to play a game of HORSE.

Tony realized I was no good at lay-ups, so he won by doing a lot of lay-ups.

It started to get dark and he wanted to keep playing but my hands were getting cold.

Mike came over today.

He said he just stopped by because he didn't have anything to do.

Then he saw Mr. Peterson and said he had to go.

(Mike's allergic to cats.)

Today Ruth came home from her job and sighed.

"I really like my job," she said, "but sometimes it's rough."

She explained a complicated story about how a supplier at the dentist's office was causing her budget problems.

She asked, "What do you think I should do?" and I didn't have any idea.

Today at the copy store I noticed Dan and Julie boxing up some copies.

They were playing a game, trying to stuff paper into the box faster than the other person.

It got to where they just crammed it in so fast that the paper got crumpled up and was flying everywhere.

Then they stopped, because they couldn't help but crack up laughing.

Today Ruth and I went to a record store.

Ruth bought a Mariah Carey CD.

"She's such a good singer," she said.

We saw a Red Hot Chili Peppers poster and Ruth said, "My sister looks like them."

Today I was hanging out at Ruth's place.

She told me to stay right where I was, and she went into the other room.

She came out with a camera and said, "Say cheese!"

But the camera didn't click, and she couldn't figure out what was wrong with it.

Steve rented "The Big Picture," which is about making Hollywood movies.

He said he liked it because he could relate to it after dabbling in show business.

Tony said, "The closest you've ever come to show biz is watching Entertainment Tonight."

Steve corrected Tony by explaining that he tried writing a script a while ago.

Today Ruth and I went to a camera repair shop.

Ruth was picking up her camera, which got repaired there.

She said it was no wonder it needed to be fixed, since it had just been sitting around collecting dust for months.

As we were leaving she said, "Now let's go buy some film."

Today at the copy store Dan was making copies.

He asked Joel how many he was supposed to make.

Joel said, "Duh," and pointed to the order slip, which says how many.

He walked away shaking his head.

Today Ruth took my picture.

Later, we went over to Steve's and took his picture.

Steve said to Ruth, "What are you, on vacation?"

She said she was just taking some pictures.

Today at work Dan was working the register.

Joel walked up to him and started talking, but I couldn't hear what they were saying.

But I heard Joel say, "Whatever, you fat little turd," when he walked away.

I noticed Dan had a scowl on his face, and all his skin was redder than usual.

Today during my lunch break at the copy store I was eating at the same time as Joel.

We weren't saying much.

Joel took a Pepsi out of the fridge and opened it.

I told him it was Dan's and he said, "So what?"

Today I worked the afternoon shift at the copy store.

I was working the register when I heard yelling and boxes being thrown in the back room.

Then I saw Dan stomp out of the store, pointing to Joel, saying, "I'm sick of your crap!"

All the customers stared, and Hal, the manager, stood there not saying anything.

I went to see Dan today.

He said, "I wonder if people are mean because of genes or environment."

I said I didn't know.

He said he tends to side with B.F. Skinner on the issue.

Today I came to work and Dan said, "Guess what."

I asked what and he told me that Joel got fired.

"There is justice in the galaxy," he said.

He went about making copies, whistling.

Today I was walking through my apartment and Mr. Peterson was standing directly in my path.

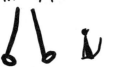

I walked right up to her and she didn't move.

So I stepped over her, one leg to each side of her.

She looked up at me and almost flipped over backwards.

I went to Ruth's place today.

She asked me over to show me something she made.

She said, "Are you ready?" and I said yes.

She turned on the light and there was a mobile hanging from her ceiling with photos of all her friends on it.

Today I decided to go visit my mom back in my hometown.

"Jim! well, hello," she said.

She told me I came just in time because she was cooking a big meal.

I went into the dining room and my grandma said, "Jim! well, hello."

(I didn't know my grandma would be there, too.)

I've been visiting my mom for a while.

Today we drove to my Aunt Harriet and Uncle Gene's farmhouse.

My mom and Aunt Harriet paired off and went to look at the garden.

Uncle Gene said to me, "So I hear you're in the copying business."

Today I went walking around by my mom's house.

Just past her house is open country.

I decided to go into one of the corn fields, even though when I was little grown-ups used to warn against walking in corn fields because it's easy to get lost in there when the stalks are really tall.

But I got out of it just fine.

Today I walked over to Julie's house.

(She was an old friend from high school.)

His mom remembered me and said, "Oh hi, Jim."

I asked her if Julie was around and she said she hasn't been home in two years.

Today it was kind of gloomy outside so I sat around and watched TV.

There was some kind of stand-up comedian on who was pretty funny.

Then nothing else was on, but I kept watching and flipping channels.

I watched until my eyes hurt.

I went over to my Dad's today.

He showed me the deck he's building behind his house.

He said, "I could use some help putting in the last few two-by-sixes."

So we spent the afternoon drilling planks, listening to the hits on his transistor radio.

I came back home today after a week at my mom's.

Mr. Peterson seemed pretty indifferent.

I put my stuff away then sat down and relaxed.

Mr. Peterson rubbed up against my leg once, then went into the other room.

Today Ruth told me she read my journal while I was gone.

She seemed kind of sad, so I asked what was the matter.

"You don't have anything in here about us getting married," she said.

"It's all... little, meaningless stuff," she said.

Today Ruth asked why I only write about little, unimportant things in my journal.

I said I didn't know why, but I just end up doing it that way.

She asked if I could at least write in something about our wedding.

I said I would.

Ruth and I got married today.

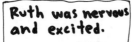

Ruth was nervous and excited.

All her relatives were there, and so were mine.

Like my mom, dad and grandma, who was wearing a pin shaped like an owl.

Today Ruth and I were just sitting around, not doing much of anything.

Ruth said, "Hey, wouldn't it be fun to drive around the country?"

I said I guess that would be a fun thing to do.

She said, "Yup." and that was all we said about it.

Today Ruth asked me, "So, when should we go on our big cross-country drive?"

I didn't realize she had seriously wanted to go, so I said, "I don't know."

She said she's been saving money from her dental lab job and would like to go right away.

I went to the copy store to tell Hal, and he said, "But Jim, now's when I need you most."

Today I told Tony that Ruth and I were planning to go on a big trip.

"Great," he said. "Just don't tell me any of the mushy details."

He said he's always wanted to go on a cross-country trip.

"Hey, can I come?" he said. "I'll just sit in back and not say anything, I promise."

Today Ruth showed me how much stuff she'd packed in her suitcase and all the routes she drew up on her maps.

She got giddy talking about all the things we could do and the places we could go.

Then I told her that Tony said he wanted to come on our trip with us.

Suddenly, and for the first time I can ever remember, Ruth wasn't smiling.

Today Tony said, "Hey Jim, you knew I was just kidding about coming on that road trip with you, right?"

Then he asked all about the trip. I told him Ruth was hoping to leave right away and be gone a few weeks.

"Jim," he said ominously, "don't you see what's going on with Ruth?"

I said no, and he whispered intensely, "she's running from the law!"

Today Ruth and I left for our big cross-country trip.

We talked for the first few hours and I started to get really tired.

When I woke up it was dark outside.

I asked Ruth where we were and she said, "Princeton, Illinois."

Today Ruth and I drove through St. Louis, Missouri.

We decided it would be fun to go to the top of the arch, so we got off the interstate into downtown.

We eventually figured out how to get to the arch entrance, and managed to find a place to park.

But the arch was closed for the day.

Ruth and I have been eating a lot of Mountain Dew and potato chips.

Today we stopped at a restaurant in Columbia, Missouri.

Ruth said, after a few bites, "This is pretty good food."

But then we decided it was about the same as food anywhere.

Today we drove through Kansas.

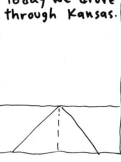

We couldn't believe that the landscape never changed, hour after hour.

We stopped so Ruth could take my picture.

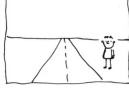

Then I took hers.

We drove through Denver today.

Ruth said, "Let's stop and look around, okay?"

So we pulled off the highway, parked, and walked around.

We went into some stores, and Ruth saw a jacket and said, "That's a great-looking jacket."

Today Ruth and I drove most of the day without stopping much.

"Jim," Ruth said, "Did you ever wonder what would've happened if we never met?"

I told her I guess I never did.

Then we got to talking about how we met, working at MacDonald's

We pulled into a truck stop today to fill up the tank and just stop and stretch.

Ruth bought some doughnuts and a funny cap.

We stood in line then paid for our stuff.

The cashier said, "You have a good day now, and may God bless you both."

Today we played the license plate ABC game for a while.

We also passed some mountains that Ruth wanted to stop and look at.

So we did.

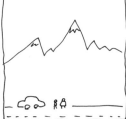

Today we were driving along the highway when a fawn jumped right in front of the car.

Ruth screamed and hit the brakes, but he appeared too suddenly and we ran right over him.

Ruth froze up, and her hands got so shaky she had to pull over.

Then she started sobbing.

Ruth hasn't been talking much.

Today we drove through Las Vegas.

I asked Ruth if she wanted to stop and see anything and she said not unless I did.

I kept driving, and noticed that every sign had fancy blinking lights on it, even the MacDonald's one.

Today Ruth and I drove into Santa Fe, New Mexico.

Ruth bought some jewelry from one of the Indian merchants on the street.

It was a ring, which she put on as soon as she bought it.

She said she couldn't believe all the stuff you could buy here.

Ruth and I have been trading off sleeping and driving.

Today we finally decided that sleeping in the car is uncomfortable.

So we stopped at a camping ground and set up Ruth's tent.

But there were so many mosquitoes and howling coyotes that it was even worse than sleeping in the car.

Today we got to Houston, Texas.

Ruth's high-school friend Tammy lives here, so we stayed at her house.

We sat in her living room and she and Ruth talked about all that's happened since high school.

Tammy had two kids, and one of them kept staring at me.

Today I was woken up by Tammy's kids playing and laughing outside my room.

It was 6am and Tammy was getting ready for work, so Ruth and I had to leave too.

Tammy thanked us for coming, and told me it was very nice meeting me.

Ruth asked what her kids were supposed to do all day and Tammy said, "oh, they'll be fine."

As we drove out of Texas, Ruth told me about her friend Tammy. "It's a sad story," she said.

She told me about how Tammy got married right after high school, then divorced after having two kids.

Then a big truck passed us on the highway and honked at us.

honk
honk

Ruth said "oop!" after noticing she was going 45 mph in the fast lane.

Today we went to Graceland.

Elvis's actual mansion was a lot smaller than we thought it would be.

"I feel faint!" a guy in the tour group said. (He was just joking.)

Then we ate in the Hound Dog Cafe, and noticed that there were a lot of flies there.

Today we stopped in Cave City, Kentucky.

Welcome to Cave City

Ruth bought a postcard to send to Steve back home.

"What should I say?" she asked me.

I said I don't know, and she stood there staring at the card.

Today we drove up the South Carolina coastline.

We stopped and ate at some beaches along the way.

"This is beautiful," Ruth said.

At one stop we watched some jet fighters put on an air show.

We drove up the east coast more today, through North Carolina and Virginia.

"I just can't believe how beautiful this is," Ruth said.

We stopped at a beach and walked along the surf.

We passed a little kid, playing with an up-turned bucket in the sand, who said, "Don't smash my castle, please."

We went on some of the Washington DC tours today.

We saw the White House, the capitol, and the Washington Monument.

I can't even remember all the things we saw.

After our tours we relaxed by the water and agreed that going on tours is pretty tiring.

Today Ruth and I got to New York City.

In Manhattan, it seemed like we were the only car that wasn't a taxi or limousine.

Ruth was really nervous driving, "because the other cars are so rude," she said.

Along the way, we noticed a funny parking sign.

Today we walked through Central Park.

It was full of a lot of people walking their dogs and their kids' strollers.

We watched the little boats on the pond for a while.

Ruth thought she saw Spike Lee, but couldn't be sure about it.

Today we roamed around New York City some more.

We walked to Times Square.

We also went to the GE Buiding because Ruth wanted to buy a David Letterman T-shirt while she still could.

Then we went to the Metropolitan Museum and saw some really old mummies.

Today we drove through Connecticut and into Massachusetts.

We drove all the way to the tip of Cape Cod.

There was an artsy fishing village there that we liked.

We stayed there for a while and ate at a restaurant on a pier, and the smell of fish was everywhere.

Today we started to head back home.

We listened to a Best of Elvis Costello tape Ruth got in Boston.

We listened to it over and over until we got sick of it.

When I took over driving, Ruth slept and mumbled something in her sleep that I couldn't make out.

Steve took care of Mr. Peterson while I was away.

"Hey, you'll never guess what Mr. Peterson likes to eat," he said.

I asked him what.

"Corn!" he said.

I went to the copy store today to tell Hal I was back.

"We could sure use you, Jim," he said.

He rubbed his forehead and said, "Things haven't been going so great around here."

Then he smiled and said, "So, how was your big trip?"

Ruth and I went to look at more apartments today.

One place didn't allow pets, another was too expensive...

"This apartment hunting is tiring," Ruth commented at one point.

After a long day of looking at apartments, we relaxed at Hardee's and ate shakes.

Today Tony asked me how married life is.

I said it was about the same.

He said, "Then why get married?"

"Got you there!" he said.

At the copy store today a man came in with an envelope.

"I'm starting a company and I need 1,500 of these," he said.

I told him we could do it but it would take almost 3 hours.

He said he'd make it worth our while.

I Feel Like a Grown-Up Now

Now we're into the most recent collection, *I Feel Like a Grown-Up Now*.

Most cartoonists opt to keep their characters the same age through the life of their comics. Bart Simpson is still a kid, after ten years on the air, and I think Dagwood and Blondie have been thirty-somethings for almost eighty years.

When I was faced with the question of whether to age Jim as I aged, or keep him perpetually young, the decision was simple. I wanted *Jim's Journal* to be a true-to-life comic strip, where Jim gets older as time goes on. But I've stopped doing the strip now, so Jim is stuck at about thirty years of age, the age when most people are hit with the sudden realization that they're grown-ups.

If by some miracle *Jim's Journal* is revived, he'll probably get older still, have kids, and turn into an old man, but I'm sure somehow his life will forever remain uneventful.

Today I was looking for a sharp pencil.

I couldn't find a single one.

So I took a pencil and sharpened it.

The smell of the lead and wood shavings almost made me sneeze.

Mr. Peterson found a twist-tie today and was playing with it.

Ruth and I went to some garage sales today.

Ruth was looking for a certain kind of placemat, but never found it.

After it started to get dark, we went home.

"Well, it was a nice day anyway," Ruth said.

The man who ordered envelopes for his new company came to the copy store today.

This time he wanted 2,000 business cards "ASAP," he said.

I told him we could get them done by tomorrow.

He said that if we did, he'd bring us all his business.

Tony called last night. He was pretty excited.

He'd just gone out with somebody to a coffee shop.

Her name is Christina, and they met at a grocery store.

"The odds of that happening have to be a million to one," Tony said.

Ruth ran into some friends of hers today.

She introduced me as her husband.

They made a big fuss over me.

I felt like a new coat or something.

It was raining this morning, so I took the bus.

The driver and an old woman were having a running conversation.

Every so often he'd stop and announce a street.

Then they'd start talking again.

At the copy store I was making change and a customer didn't get it.

She said I wasn't giving her enough back.

I showed her the receipt and counted it out again.

She pretended to be satisfied, but I could tell she thought I counted it wrong.

I took a nap today.

I got up really slowly.

Ruth is moving our furniture all around.

She's putting things on top of things.

She's putting lamps around in places I never would've thought.

Tonight she finished and said, "Isn't that better?"

I made a wiener for lunch today.

I don't eat wieners a lot, but sometimes I just have to.

I diced some onions and put them on with brown mustard.

It was pretty good.

Mr. Peterson doesn't pay me as much attention anymore.

She likes Ruth.

Her favorite is to make a nest in her lap.

She turns around and around, pushing down, then lies down.

Tony brought his new friend Christina to the copy store today.

"Stay away from Jim," he told her. "He knows all my secrets."

We all laughed and then they left.

He came back later and asked, "So what did you think?"

I came home tonight and couldn't find Mr. Peterson anywhere.

I turned the place upside-down looking for her.

I found her inside a bathroom cabinet.

"How did you get in there?" I said.

Somebody came into the store today and wanted us to copy a whole book.

I told her it would be cheaper to just buy another book.

Then Hal came over and said we couldn't do it anyway.

She came back three or four hours later but left right away.

I brought in the mail today.

There was some junk mail for Ruth.

Before her name was "Mrs."

"That's kinda nice," she said.

Tony had me help him move his couch today. 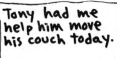	"A little cleaning is good for the soul, Jim," he said. 	There were clots of dust underneath it. 	Tony said, "Oh, man!"
I was just sitting around today. 	Then I went to work. 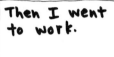	Then I came home and made a jelly sandwich. 	Ruth said, "Jim, are you a 'slacker?'" 
Today Ruth asked if I ever thought of taking up a hobby. 	I said I guess I never did. 	She said I should take one up, "Like maybe stamp collecting," she said. 	Then she said it didn't have to be stamp collecting, it could be anything. 
We were talking about copies at the copy store today. 	We tried to come up with our craziest customer story. 	Everybody had a story about an unusual incident. 	Hal, the manager, said, "You know, it's the people that make this job worthwhile." 

I ran into Tony's friend Christina on the street today.

We talked a bit and then walked our separate ways.

Tony called tonight and said he'd heard about our bumping into each other.

"Did she say anything about me?" he asked, kind of desperately.

I always thought I was a pretty tidy person.

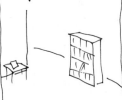

But everything is extra neat now that Ruth lives with me.

Sometimes I forget how things must have been before.

I must have been pretty much a complete slob.

I sat outside on my break today.

A squirrel came right up close to me.

First he'd look at me with one eye, then the other.

I'd never seen such a friendly squirrel.

Tony and Christina came over last night.

We watched TV and ate popcorn.

Tony and I talked a little, but Christina didn't join in.

When they left she hugged me and said, "Thanks, Jim."

Ruth and I went to a hobby shop today.

We bought some stamps and a stamp album.

We also got a little envelope of paper hinges to hold the stamps in.

Ruth asked the clerk, "There's a lot to this, isn't there?"

I was standing behind some people at a stoplight today.

"She's the dumbest smart woman I know," said the woman.

The man said, "No, you know dumber smart people."

The odd thing was that I knew exactly what they meant.

Today I was making change for a customer and got confused.

"No, that's right," she said. "One more five and we'll be square."

I gave her one more five, the way she said.

I had no idea if it was right or not.

Today I saw some kids play- ing football.

They were yelling and having a good time.

There were boys and girls playing.

They had some friends on the side who just watched.

Ruth and I ate out with Tony and Christina tonight.

Ruth had a salad and I had lasagna.

Tony had a garibaldi sandwich and Christina had a small pizza.

After we were done, Ruth said, "This is nice."

Ruth and I rented a movie last night.

It was about a man who meets a woman in World War II. It was pretty good.

The phone rang and we paused the tape while I answered it.

When we started it up again it didn't seem as good as before.

Today I noticed Mr. Peterson over in the corner.

There was a tiny bug walking up the wall, and Mr. Peterson looked up at it and squeaked.

The bug started coming down, and she put her paw on it like she was squashing it.

But when she took her paw away, the bug started walking up again.

I was really tired tonight, so I went to bed early.

After a few hours I woke up and felt fine.

I watched TV and had something to eat.

I went to bed again around 3, but I didn't feel the least bit sleepy.

For some reason it was really busy at the copy store today.

There were forms, flyers, resumes, everything.

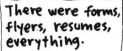

One person even brought in a calendar for 2 years from now.

"You have to plan ahead," she said.

Today I did the laundry.

After drying, I separated my stuff from Ruth's.

Then I folded them.

Today I made myself a pot pie.

I sat down to eat it and Mr. Peterson came up and watched.

Every time I would lift my fork, she would reach out and put her paw on my hand.

I looked at her and she let out a big meow.

Today Steve came over.

He said he found a basket just lying around his apartment, and that he didn't need it and wondered if I'd take it.

I said sure.

So now I have the basket.

I went to the grocery store today and saw they had pumpkins.

There were long ones, huge ones, ugly ones and tiny ones

I didn't buy one or anything.

Then Ruth came home and surprised me with a pumpkin.

Today I was picking some stuff up in my room.

In a pile by my desk I found all the stamp-collecting things Ruth got for me, unopened.

I thought of Ruth going to the trouble of getting it for me as a gift.

I felt bad that I wasn't really interested in it.

Today I watched Mr. Peterson discover the basket that Steve brought over.

She sniffed it for a second, then got right into it and sat down.

It was just the right size for her.

She licked her paw a little, then went right to sleep.

Ruth called today and asked what I was doing for Halloween.

I told her I didn't know.

She said we should at least rent a scary movie.

I said that sounded fine.

Tony called today and invited me to a Halloween party.

It's going to be at his girlfriend Christina's.

"Everybody's coming," he said. "wear a costume."

The rest of the day I tried to think of a costume I could wear.

Today I thought about what I'd wear to Tony and Christina's Halloween party.

I thought about being Mr. Peterson.

Or a piece of paper.

Or Deputy Secretary of Weights and Measures Michael Stemens.

I still don't know what I'll be.

I have a new game to play with Mr. Peterson.

when she's in her basket I scratch the outside of it.

She reaches out and tries to get my finger.

She never gets tired of this game.

Tony called today to cancel the Halloween party.

He was going to have it with his girlfriend, Christina.

"she's going through something, I don't know," he said.

I didn't know what to say.

Ruth and I rented a scary movie today.

She wanted to watch one for Halloween.

It was a pretty good movie. (It was "Christine," the evil car movie.)

But neither of us got very scared or anything.

I was taking my shoes off and I noticed little pieces of leaves on my socks.

I didn't know how they got in there.

I was going to pick off each piece and throw it away.

But I just put the socks in the laundry with the leaves on them.

Last night Tony and I watched TV.

It was a show about aliens and a government cover-up.

At the end, the two investigators weren't any closer to the truth.

"So, do you think Christina is the right girl for me?" Tony asked.

Ruth came home early today.

She saw that I haven't done much with all the stamp collecting stuff she got for me.

She said, "I guess you haven't had time to try it yet."

I said I guess so.

I think Mr. Peterson is having trouble with my being married.

She's used to sleeping with me at night.

But now there isn't always room for her.

Today I got a big envelope from my grandma.

It was full of stamps for my collection.

She must have been saving them for years.

I put them with my other stamp stuff, which I still haven't used.

Today I wrote to my grandma.

I really should write to her more often.

Today when I came home I accidentally stepped on Mr. Peterson's paw.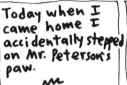

She made a loud shriek and ran into the other room.

I felt bad and ran after her, but I think I only made her more scared.

When I got to her, she was hiding in the closet, almost too scared to let me touch her.

I was cleaning out my closet today.

I found an old school transcript.

It had a list of almost every class I took that year.

It's hard to believe I did all that work.

When I got up today I noticed Mr. Peterson was still in the closet.

I guess it's her new favorite spot.

When I got outside I could see my breath, and the exhaust from cars.

Everything seemed more crisp, even the sound.

Tony called today to see if I wanted to go to a movie with him.

I said that Ruth wanted to stay in tonight.

"Ruth wants to stay in?!" he said.

Then he said, "You're whipped!"

Ruth came home today to work on my stamp collection.

She brought along a lot of envelopes that her grandpa had, with foreign stamps on them.

We soaked them in a bowl of water.

After a while the stamps came loose.

Hal called us all around at the copy store today.

After thinking about it, he said he'd come to a decision.

We would be closed for Thanksgiving.

We pretty much had assumed that all along.

Today at the copy store I was loading paper in one of the self-service machines.

Hal, the manager, was working at the cash register.

I heard him say to a customer, "...and 64 cents is your change. You have a good day now.."

Then another customer came up to him and he said, "Hi, what can I do for you today?"

Ruth and I drove to her folks for Thanksgiving today.

When we got there, her dad asked us which way we'd come.

He also wanted to know how the traffic had been.

Ruth's sister was looking at me from behind her mom.

Ruth's dad asked me if I'd give him a hand this morning.

We raked some leaves, with the radio on.

It was playing a football game.

One time, when one of the teams fumbled, he said, "Oh, crud."

Ruth drove us home from her parents' today.

She made me take lots of leftovers.

I didn't really want them, but I said thanks.

Tony had come by and left lots of food for Mr. Peterson.

I washed a load of clothes today.

I didn't have anything else to do today, so I just sat in the basement laundry room and waited.

Before I put my clothes in the dryer I emptied the lint filter, which is my favorite part of doing laundry.

When I brought the clothes back up to the apartment, Mr. Peterson jumped on top of them and got comfortable.

It snowed last night.

On the sidewalk you could see all the footprints.

Most were tennishoes, but some were different.

Somebody had made really long tracks by sliding.

Ruth went shopping today.

We stopped and she had me try on some pants.

I also tried on sweaters, ties, and even some shoes with little bells on the laces.

We never did get anything for her.

This morning Ruth said, "You could wear your suit today."

I had the day off.

So I did.

This morning I looked for my gloves.

I hadn't worn them since last winter.

I couldn't find them. I did find my mittens, though.

When Tony saw me wearing them he said "Ha! Mittens!"

Ruth called from work and said "I have an idea."

She wanted to come home and eat pizza and work on my stamp collection.

I said okay, but she seemed disappointed.

I guess she thought I'd be really excited.

Someone left their original on one of the copiers at the store today.

It was in some kind of foreign writing.

None of us could guess what language it was.

Hal said to hold on to it.

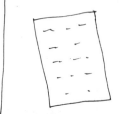

I found a $5 bill in the copy store today.

Hal said I could keep it unless someone came in to claim it.

No one ever claimed it.

It made me feel sort of guilty, but also good.

Ruth says she knows just what to get me.

I told her I really don't need anything.

"You won't believe it! It's perfect," she said.

I have no idea what it could be.

At work today a woman struck up a conversation with me.

She was in her 40's, and had just moved to town.

We were copying her resume.

"We should get together sometime," she said.

The woman I met yesterday was in again.

She wanted envelopes with her name on them but no address.

"I might move if things don't work out," she said.

"My name is Nadine. What's yours?" she said.

My dad called me at work today.

He wanted to know what my holiday plans were.

I didn't really know.

"Well, keep me posted," he said.

At work today Hal, the manager, was upset.

He had us clean just about everything.

When it was all over, he left the store.

He came back with malted milks for everybody.

I think Ruth is going to get me a big present. 	She's being really secretive. 	I guess it will be a big surprise. 	
I went to mail some letters today. 	I noticed a big display on stamp collecting. 	I told the clerk about Ruth getting me into stamps. 	"Stamp collecting is a post office marketing ploy," she said. 
At the copy store a woman wanted a lot of help. 	She wanted two sheets of about 15 kinds of paper. 	What she really wanted was a kind of paper none of us had ever heard of.	"What's the matter with you people?" she said. 
Ruth came home last night and gave me her present. 	She was really excited as I opened it. 	It was a video on stamp collecting. 	I thanked her for it, and we watched it. 

Steve came over today to get my keys.

He's going to take care of Mr. Peterson while I'm away.

He played with Mr. Peterson for a while and called her "old timer."

I'm at my mom's house. We had lots of relatives over today.

After eating we got out scrapbooks.

I looked at pictures of me from when I was little.

Some of them were pretty funny.

I took a bath today.

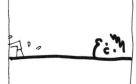

My mom has a really big tub.

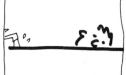

I can read or soak for a long time.

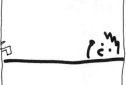

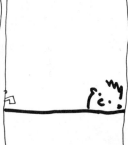

Ruth called today to see how my visit to my mom's was going.

I said it was pretty good.

She said her trip was, too.

"Yup," she said. "Yeeup."

I came home today. 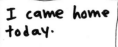	Mr. Peterson was very happy. 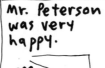	We played for a while. 	It looked like Steve had worked on my stamp collection while I was gone. 
Nadine was in the copy shop today. 	I asked her if she needed anything. 	She said, "No, I just wanted to say hi." 	It felt sort of weird. 
Sometimes I don't mind doing dishes. 	Most times I don't want to do them and let them pile up. 	But when I do them, it's not so bad and I feel good at the end. 	Other times I just go as fast as I can. 
Today at the copy store Dan and I were talking. 	"There's probably lots better jobs than this," he said. 	We sat around and tried to think of better jobs. 	"Seismologist," he said. 

I walked by a car accident today. 	It was on the other side of the street. 	Everyone was trying to see it. 	I thought maybe I shouldn't look, but I did. 
Nadine found out I have a cat today. 	She said she has four. 	She told me all about them. 	Then she said she wants to meet Mr. Peterson. 
Today was garbage day. 	You could see lots of gift wrappings in the bags. 	There were a lot of trees, too. 	There was a lot of garbage. 
I got my hair cut today. 	I thought it was pretty short. 	"Looks fine to me," Ruth said. 	When I washed my hair it felt weird. 

It's still really cold outside.	It makes for more static electricity.	We have lots more paper jams because of it.	It seems like all I did today was take out paper jams.

I was bored tonight.	I called everybody I knew, but no one was home.	finally I started a book.	Tony came over and wanted to go skating, but by then I was into my book.

At the copy store today I was working with Dan.	He asked how long I'd worked here.	I said two or three years, I guess.	He thought that was pretty funny.

Today Ruth and I were just sitting around.	I was reading a newspaper.	Ruth decided it would be fun to bake some cookies.	I suddenly felt like a grown-up.

| It snowed last night.  | I made a snow-ball and threw it at a stop sign.  | It missed. | It wasn't a big deal, but I still looked around to see if anyone noticed.  |

| I was sitting around reading today.  | Mr. Peterson was sitting on the shelf, looking out the window.  | Then she stood up and looked intently out-side.  | I guess there was something really interesting happening.  |

Today Hal said, "I hear you're looking for a new job."

I told him I hadn't thought about it.

"Well, good then," he said, and he walked away.

Then I thought maybe I should look for a new job.

It snowed today.

Everybody was driving slowly.

It made it hard to cross the street.

When I got home my shoes and socks were wet.

I stopped by Ruth's work today. She's a dental hygienist.

I saw that she'd brought all our old magazines to the waiting room.

There were all sorts of strangers reading my magazines.

It was kind of weird.

Steve and I went to lunch today.

We went to a Mexican restaurant.

They gave us lots of chips and salsa while we waited.

When the food finally came we were already full.

Nadine came in today.

She talked for a long time.

I kept starting different tasks, but she never left.

She didn't seem to notice I was busy.

Today Tony said I had to come look at something.

I went to his apartment and Steve was there too.

"Ta-da!" he said, as he showed us a computer on his desk.

"Welcome to the 1980's," Steve said.

Today I moved my shelf away from the window.

Mr. Peterson used to sit on the shelf and look outside, and she tried to stand up and look out, but wasn't tall enough.

Once she even jumped up on the window sill, but it was too thin and she fell off.

So I put the shelf back.

I was at Tony's today.

He was excited because he just went on-line.

He started downloading pictures of actresses from Baywatch.

"This is the future, Jim," he said.

Ruth wants to start exercising.

She's joining a health club to do weights.

She also wants to start jogging.

"You could use it too," she said.

I fell today.

I landed right on my tail-bone.

Nadine came to the store and I told her about it.

"Oh, you poor thing," she said.

We watched TV tonight and Ruth put her head in my lap.

It wasn't very comfortable.

Tony called me at the copy store today.

He said, "Jim—fast! How do you spell astronaut?"

I did my best to spell it, then he repeated it back.

He said, "Gotta run. Thanks, pal!"

Today I told Hal I was looking for a different job.

He said, "Good luck to you, Jim."

I guess I thought it would be a bigger deal.

Ruth and I went jogging today.

Today Tony told me all about the space shuttle missions.

"Did you know there's humans up in space right this second?" he said.

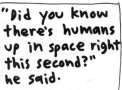

"That's amazing," he said. "In outer space!"

A few minutes later he said it again. "In outer space!"

As I was leaving work today, I ran into Nadine.

She said we should go out for coffee.

We went in her car and drove for a while.

It was a really expensive car, I think.

It's getting warmer.

Today there was that muddy smell.

I called Ruth to see if she wanted to jog again.

She said she would, but that she needed to heal up.

Ruth got home early last night. We were going to make dinner.

On our way to the grocery store, we talked about jobs I could apply for.

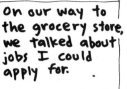

I've seen want ads for bank tellers, insurance and advertising sales.

When we got to the store Ruth said, "You could work here!"

Three girls came into the copy store today.

They were wearing high-school letter jackets from a town I didn't know.

They looked at all the supplies and laughed a lot.

I guess they had never seen a copy store before.

Tony said he read an article about becoming an astronaut.

"I'm serious about this, Jim," he said. "I really am."

He wants to go to Mars, maybe beyond, even though the trip would take years.

"But it said I'd have to go back to school," he said. "I don't know."

I told Tony I was probably going to find a different job.

He said, "Have you considered astronaut, Jim?"

"They get to travel and wear cool suits, and I bet they get tons of babes."

I told him I was thinking of the grocery store and he said, "Babes, babes and more babes."

I was really tired at work today.

When I got off, I was going right home for a nap.

I walked home as fast as I could.

When I got home, I didn't feel the least bit sleepy.

Ruth and I talked today.

I told her Steve and I were going to work on my resume.

I told her I didn't know how to write one to get a good job.

She said, "For hobbies, put stamp collecting."

Today Tony gave me some tips on how to write resumes and cover letters.

"I know how to do all that crap," he said.

He said you have to use action words in your resume.

And he showed me exactly how you fold a cover letter.

steve and I worked on a resume for me all day.

I listed McDonald's, the book store and the copy store.

steve looked at it up and down.

"Rennaisance man," he said.

Tonight I turned on the TV and wheel of fortune was on.

I watched it for a while and was going to switch channels.

But there really was no good reason to.

I watched it all the way to the end.

I was over at Tony's to see his computer again.

We looked up a movie on the internet. First we logged on, then found a "search engine."

Then we clicked on "Entertainment," then movies, then an alphabetical list.

The movie we wanted wasn't listed.

Ruth came into the copy store today.

She said, "I haven't seen you much lately."

I said I guess I'd been busy.

Nadine happened to come in at that moment and they met.

Tony called me tonight.

He said he and Christina were back together.

I hadn't known they'd broken up.

He said, "Jim, are you blind?"

Today Ruth was sitting by my stamp collecting stuff.

She sort of rubbed her face a little, and I could tell she was crying.

"I'm no good at buying presents," she said. "Because you don't like stamp collecting, do you?"

I tried to console her and tell her it was no big deal.

I think I need new socks.

The ones I have are getting thin, and with the snow they get wet fast.

Every morning I plan to get new ones.

But then I forget all about it until the next day.

I mailed out a resume today.

I made sure to fold it so that the top was a quarter inch over the fold.

That's what Tony said to do.

I wondered about a person who would be offended if I folded it wrong.

Tony and I went out for pancakes today.

He didn't like his and left part.

The waitress came and asked how things were.

Tony said, "Fine."

I got a call today for a job interview at a bank.

I went in and they gave me coffee.

The vice president asked what I thought I could offer them.

I said I really didn't know.

I went to the grocery store today to fill out an application.

The manager looked at it and asked if I could start Monday.

I got the job without even showing my resume.

When I got home I called Tony and he said, "You loser."

Today Mr. Peterson was sleeping under my blanket.

I didn't notice at first, but when I sat on the bed she squeaked.

Then she stuck her head out to see what was going on.

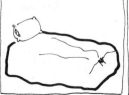

The way the blanket was wrinkled, it looked like she had a huge bed-sized body and a little head.

This is the grocery store where I work now.

It's just four aisles, but there seems to be everything.

Today a woman asked me where candles were.

I looked everywhere and then she said, "Wait, we're right in front of them!"

Steve was playing on his computer today, sending e-mail to Tony.

"It's so much faster than the post office," he said. "And cheaper."

I asked him if he'd ever write to Tony at all if it weren't for e-mail.

"Not under any circumstance," he said.

At the store today I was putting crayons on the shelf.

They smelled so good I stopped and opened a box.

I hadn't smelled that smell for a long time.

Then I saw a customer watching and I went back to work.

Today Tony told me he and Steve have been e-mailing each other.

He said, "And you should hear what we're saying about you, Jim." Then he laughed.

Suddenly he got really loud and said, "Respond, dammit! That was funny."

I was stocking today and looked closely at Chef Boyardee.

I wondered if he was real.

If he is, he must be retired by now.

Mr. Peterson knows I've changed jobs.

Something at the grocery store must smell good to her.

I don't know what she smells, but it's on my pants cuffs.

I tried to smell what she does, but I couldn't detect anything.

It snowed last night, the light fluffy kind.

This morning everything was quiet.

But I could hear my footsteps.

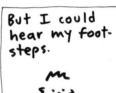

Every time I took a step, it sounded like a wet balloon.

Today Mr. Peterson was sprawled out on the floor in the sun ray from the window.

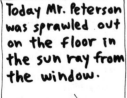

She was so far asleep that when I walked by she didn't even move.

Normally she's startled by the slightest thing, but I nudged her and she only twitched her leg.

Tony came over last night and we ordered a pizza.

We got just about everything on it, even pineapple.

When we ate it, Tony said, "This pizza rules!"

Then he said, "No, this pizza rocks!"

Mr. Peterson cleaned herself then got comfy in the window's sun ray today.

After an hour or so, the sun ray moved, and Mr. Peterson wasn't inside it anymore.

She got up and stretched.

Then she moved over to where the ray was and fell asleep again.

Today Harry, the store butcher, showed me how the beef grinder works.

He put in fat trimmings, steaks that were brown, lots of things.

When it came out it looked perfectly good.

"Behold, Jim," he said. "I've taken something you might throw away and I've made it beautiful."

I got a post card from my grandma today.

She's visiting Arizona.

She said she's having a good time.

"Maybe next time you can come along," she said.

I got a call tonight from a long-distance company.

They asked me to switch. They said they missed serving me. They had "21 reach-out reasons to come home," and gave me $20.

I said okay.

I really don't care who my phone company is.

Ruth asked me to bring some things home from the store today.

She needed things I never would have guessed.

Rubbing alcohol, cotton balls, mineral oil, baby oil.

For myself I got chips.

I broke my shoelace this morning.

I went out and got some new ones. When I put them in, they almost glowed, they were so white.

All day I felt like people were staring at my bright feet.

A married couple was in the store today.

After they left, Harry said, "Ever notice how couples over time start to look like each other?"

I thought about Ruth.

Ruth and I rented a video tonight. 	It was a Sandra Bullock movie. 	After it was over, Ruth asked, "Do you think she's prettier than me?" 	I said no.

Steve came over today and we were looking at Mr. Peterson conked out and belly-up in the sun ray. 	"The sun must be like some kind of cat drug," steve said. 	"Maybe you should get her some treatment," he said. 	"Kitty rehab," he said. Then he laughed. Then he cleared his throat. Then there was an awkward pause in the conversation.

Today I walked home with Betsy, who works at the grocery store. 	We ran into Tony. 	"Hey," he said, "I was just going to get me a burger. wanna come?" 	Betsy said she doesn't eat meat, and that when her grandpa died they found 10 lbs of rotten meat in his colon.

Tony came into the store today. 	I showed him all the meat Harry cut. 		"That's kinda gross," he said. 

The shelves at the store are really high.

To reach things, sometimes you have to use this tool.

It has pincers on the end.

It's one of my favorite things to do.

Ruth brought home a bird house kit today.

She said I could build it so Mr. Peterson can watch the birds.

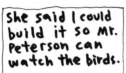

"It only cost 40 dollars," she said.

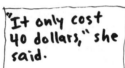

"And it will give you and Mr. Peterson something to do.

Ruth had me help her bring in some groceries today.

She'd bought a 100 pound bag of birdseed.

There were cartoon drawings of cardinals on it.

It was heavy.

One of the guys I work with, Ernie, is in a band.

"We're trying to recreate that '70s sound," he said.

"Smooth, elegant, and suave."

He said the name of the band is Groove Bootie.

I opened a new bar of soap yesterday.

Today it had already melted so the writing on it was very faint.

I thought maybe I should get a different kind of soap, but I didn't know which.

Then I realized I had no idea why I got my regular soap in the first place.

"I'm becoming a vegetarian," Tony said today.

"It just came to me," he said. "It's the right way to live."

We went to McDonald's and he ordered a 20-piece McNuggets.

Tony looked at us and said, "There's no way chicken counts."

This morning Ruth watched the birds at our new feeder.

"They're hardly eating anything," she said.

Today Harry was cutting up a chicken.

Then he cut up some sandwich meat for a customer.

I asked him if he shouldn't have washed his hands first.

"Oh, a college man!" he said.

Ruth came into the store today.

I introduced her to Harry.

We talked for a bit, then Ruth left.

Harry came up to me and said, "Wow, she's a looker!"

Tonight I was watching TV and noticed some soap ads.

I thought of maybe changing soaps.

There's one that doesn't leave a sticky film.

If it smells okay I might try it.

Ruth said she's thinking of changing her hair.

She asked my opinion but I really didn't have one.

"Well, it might be drastic, so I don't want to hear any complaints," she said.

She's thinking of getting a pony tail.

Ernie brought in a tape of his band today.

"We recorded it at our coffeehouse gig," he said.

On the tape, the music was kind of muffled and there were people talking.

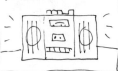

"That'll all come out in the mix," he said.

Tony came to the store today. "Feast your eyes on this," he said.

He showed me a photo he got from an actress he wrote to.

She signed the photo, but we couldn't make out what she wrote.

"But still," Tony said. He winked and made a clicking noise with his tongue.

Ruth was making grilled-cheese sandwiches tonight.

She noticed Mr. Peterson looking out the window.

She dropped her spatula and ran to the window yelling, "Mr. Peterson is looking at the bird house!"

Mr. Peterson got startled from all the noise and ran away.

Tony came over tonight.

He had a People magazine.

It talked about Alex, the actress he likes, and her female lover.

"I was too late, Jim." he said.

Ruth is really having trouble with her hair.

She wants to change it, but doesn't know how.

She could get a perm, or even be blonde, she says.

"It's hard," she said today, "I have such a long face, you know."

I heard a loud bang in the other room today. 	I looked and saw a plant on the floor that had been high on a shelf. 	Mr. Peterson was hiding. 	She must have done it, but I couldn't imagine how she got up there.
Ruth brought over some pictures of hair styles she might get. 	She was thinking maybe a Jennifer Anniston look. 		"Do you think?" Ruth said. 
Today a customer brought back some chips. 	I asked if they'd gone bad. 	He said, "No, I just don't like the taste." 	There was only about a third left in the bag. 
We got squirt guns in the store today. 	Ernie filled one up with water. 	He shot it over an aisle and hit Harry. 	"What the hell is going on?" Harry yelled. 

Ruth wanted to know if I think she'd look better as a blonde.

I said I didn't know.

She didn't seem very happy with that.

"I wish you'd take this seriously!" she said.

I woke up today and didn't know if it was today or not.

I thought maybe it was tomorrow already.

Then I remembered that I had only taken a nap.

Also, I was fully dressed, so I figured that it must be today.

My mom sent me a letter today.

Ruth said "You should write her back."

I told her maybe I would eventually.

Later I saw Ruth writing a letter to my mom.

I ran into Tony today.

He was eating an apple.

"I'm so healthy, Jim. Vegetarian eating is a snap," he said.

"This is, like, the twentieth apple I've eaten today," he said.

 Today someone came in looking for bok choy.

 I said I didn't think we had any.

 She said, "Well, I'll have to go somewhere else, then, won't I?"

 I couldn't think of anything to say to that.

 Tony and Ruth and Steve and I got together tonight.

 Ruth said she was having a hard time deciding on a hair style.

 Steve told her, "It's what's on the inside that counts, Ruth."

 "Ha!" Tony said.

Ruth showed me her new hair style today.

I didn't notice anything different at first.

She finally had to explain it.

It's a pony tail.

I took a bath today.

Mr. Peterson sat on the edge and appeared to be fascinated.

Once in a while she would slap the water.

one time the water splashed back at her and she took off running.

"Being a vegetarian is hard," Tony said today.

"I mean, after you cut out hamburgers, what's left?"

He microwaved some hot dogs.

"I know hot dogs are technically meat, but I'm putting chili on 'em. And chili has beans," he said.

Tony saw a penny on the sidewalk today.

Ruth said not to pick it up.

"If it's heads, you get a wish, but tails is bad luck," she said.

"That was a close one," Tony said.

Ruth says she is going to start her own journal.

She said she looked forward to growing as a person.

"It will be all about _you_," she said.

Ruth got a special book for her journal.

It's a scrapbook, but she's adding details.

She used Elmer's glue and sequins and wrote out "Ruth's Journal" on the cover.

"I see why you enjoy keeping a journal so much," she said.

Ruth asked today if I would read her journal.

She's kept it only 2 days but has written 19 pages.

"I have so much to write about," she said.

"Tomorrow I'm doing love, wednesday is God and Thursday is food."

Tony and Steve came over tonight.

We ordered a pizza.

There was nothing good on TV.

After a while Ruth said, "Hey. let's all read my journal."

Ruth had me read her journal today.

The first day she'd written 12 pages, the second she wrote 7.

The third day she wrote 3 pages and the fourth she wrote just a sentence or 2.

I guess she hadn't gotten around to writing today's yet.

Some of Jennifer's kids were in the store today.

She was too busy to talk to them much.

They helped me stock some lettuce, which was nice.

They wanted to know if they'd get paid.

We have lots of Coke at the store.

We have Coke, Cherry Coke and Classic Coke.

We have diet Coke, decaf Coke, and decaf diet Coke.

That is a lot of Coke.

Last week I moved one of my plants.

All of a sudden it doesn't look like it's doing very well.

Ruth took a look at it.

"I sing to the plants," she said.

Ruth said I should sing to my sick plant.

I cleared my throat to get ready to sing a song.

Even before I started, Mr. Peterson looked at me like I was crazy.

I decided not to go through with it.

I got my bike out today and got it ready to ride again.

I took it down to the bike shop where there's a free air hose.

They had lots of unusual bikes there — low ones, long ones.

I'd put them down, but bikes are hard for me to draw.

Tony and I watched a movie tonight. It was Citizen Kane.

The paper said it's a movie about "a man who sacrifices his principles, sowing his own misfortune."

Tony ordered a sausage pizza, and I reminded him he was a vegetarian.

"Screw that!" he said, and continued ordering the pizza.

Today Ruth and I came in to find Mr. Peterson sleeping on my plant.

Ruth said, "Mr. Peterson, you shouldn't be sleeping in all that dirt."

She lifted Mr. Peterson out and put her on the floor.

Mr. Peterson let out a little squawk.

There is a man who comes to the store who is visiting from Russia.

Every time he buys a different kind of cigarettes.

He talks and talks about cigarettes. I guess they're a big treat for him.

I asked him if he's going to stay in America, and he said he would like to very much.

Tony has a beret.

He pointed it out to me by leaning his head down and saying, "Huh...? Huh?"

Later, we met up with Ruth.

Tony said, "Huh...? Huh?"

I was sitting around at home today.

I noticed Mr. Peterson sleeping in my plant again.

She looked really comfortable.

I decided it was no big deal, so I just left her there.

Today a customer asked Harry if the steaks were fresh.

He said, "No, they're spoiled. We want to poison you."

They both had a good laugh over that.

After the customer left, Harry said under his breath, "Nitwit."

Tony really likes his new beret.

So does Ruth.

"Maybe Jim and I should get berets too," she said.

Tony said, "Oh, man. That would ruin it!"

I had a weird dream last night.

I dreamt I could fly.

I saw a building on fire, and I flew over to it.

But the only super power I had was flying, so it burned down.

Ruth came into the store today.

She said I should consider groceries as a career.

"We could open our own store," she said.

"Jim and Ruth's!"

I need a haircut.

The grocery store is next to a salon, and they're there all day and all night, it seems.

They wear lots of jewelry and their hair is purple or green sometimes.

They said they would cut my hair for free if they could experiment.

I have a couple pairs of tenni-shoes.

one pair looked really bad.

I figured I had nothing to lose, so I put them in the washing machine.

when they came out, they looked better than my newest pair.

Tony came over today.

we were going to hang out for a while.

Ruth saw me off, saying, "I love you, Jim."

After we left, Tony said, "Jim, watch out. That Ruth chick is up to something."

It was really warm today, so Ruth and I walked to the zoo.

The bison was out.

That was about it, though.

We could have gone inside and looked at snakes, but Ruth said she did not want to have anything to do with snakes.

Ruth and I went for a walk.

It's really sunny these days.

Ruth saw me squinting and said I should get some sun-glasses.

We stopped at a place and tried some on.

Tonight I got some bags out for Mr. Peterson. 	She likes to hide inside them and poke the end. 	Sometimes she makes the bag roll over. 	She had a pretty good time. 
Mr. Peterson was sleeping on the couch today. 	She was curled up in a tight little ball. 	I stuck my finger in the tight space between her hand and her chin. 	She didn't move or wake up or anything, so I kept it there.